Now is the Time

Now is the Time

A story of abuse overcome by faith.

Lee Spotts

All Song Lyrics are quoted from Musixmatch. With credit to the Artist.

Scripture Quotations are from:
The Holy Bible, King James Version, Tyndale 1526

Also Quoted:
Holy Bible, New International Version (NIV) Zondervan 1984

Cover Image ID: 109393479
Copyright Wave Break Media Ltd | Dreamstime.com
https://www.dreamstime.com/vectorfusionart_info

Dedication

To my loving husband, "My Speed Racer", and my three beautiful children. Love you to the Moon infinite.

Abuse can be physical, sexual, emotional, verbal, or a combination of any or all of these. Abuse can also be neglect, which is when a caregiver does not take care of the basic needs of the individual who is dependent on them.

If you are experiencing abuse of any kind reach out to your local abuse hotline.

Table Of Contents

Foreword

Dear Reader,

I want to start by saying this is not a book or a story; you are being invited to join in on an *"Experience."* These memoirs are a chronological account of specific events and not a full depiction of the journey walked. There will be times when you will be asked to break from the memoir, and invited to listen to a song that encapsulates the emotional moments tied to the reading. My hope is that the lyrics to these hand-selected songs will enhance your experience and help you gain a greater spiritual connection. Now before you put this book down assuming it is another God book, wait, keep reading. The pages will reveal the story of a young girl who found hope, strength, and peace through trials and tribulations. You will be drawn into her world, see her heart, and see what God did in the midst of a life that looked like it was destined for tragedy.

Previously, when I tried to fulfill "**MY**" destiny, and put "**MY**" thoughts on paper, "**I**" struggled to even begin. Everything was jumbled and "**I**" had no idea where to start. Over the years, whenever *"I"* tried to write things down, all "**I**" heard from that voice, the voice I had come to depend on in my life, was "NOT YET."

Over time the answer became clear. The "**MY**" and the "**I**" had to be removed from the story. The story is His because He was there the whole time. He was there before "**I**" was born; He is the one that allowed the story to come to fruition. Today, while reading scriptures and listening to worship music it came to me: "**The Time is Now!**" **Do it NOW!**" Well, one thing "**I**" have learned is that when He speaks, I need to listen. So, I picked up my laptop and began to write. The pages that follow flowed out, in 6 days, as a confirmation that the timing of **Now** was indeed His direction. He poured 25 pages out of me in less than a day, 50 the next, and 100 the next. It was effortless. He also led the writing of this journey to be in 3rd person. At first "**I**" kept creeping in. I wondered why I was led to the third person. The answer came through clear as a bell. Writing this journey in 3rd person took out the "**MY**". In addition, it made it easier to revisit the pain these memories invoked from the distance of the third person.

Introduction

Have you ever had the premise that you were meant to do
something, but the timing wasn't right? You just never felt the
passion to make it happen? Like it was stuck? Yet you knew that
someday you were destined to do it? There have been two callings
in my life that have resonated in my soul. The first came to me in
1972, when I was eight years old. I was to adopt a child, not just any
child, a child that would be saved from a life of abuse, and that was
to be racially different from me. The second was that I was to share
the journey that led me here. This story is filled with abuse, pain,
amazing love, and miracles. The first calling came to fruition 17
years ago in 2006. My husband and I adopted my daughter Grace,
an interracial child who was destined for a life of abuse.

The second has just begun. Fulfilling this second calling
required me to reach into the well-stashed storage place and open
memories that have been concealed and stifled so that I could share
them with whomever God leads to the experience. The goal of this
reading and listening experience is to show others the difference that
God can make in their lives even if it seems like they have been
dealt a bad hand. There is hope and there is no such thing as a bad
hand. There are just different journeys that lead us to complete the
work we were destined to fulfill. The reading/listening experience
was composed to show how He can bless like no other. How He can

give peace like no other. How He can provide a way like no other. How He can change a situation just when you have lost all hope, like no other. He gives us our purpose, and we are meant to carry it out. He holds us together like glue. He is our Laminin. What does one have to do to tap into the power this knowledge affords? It's simply a choice, swap your will for His will. Choose His way, not your way. Who is He? His name is Jesus.

Check out this 5 min video by Louie Giglio on YouTube about Laminin. It will change your thinking about life as you know it. *https://www.youtube.com/watch?v=QSR8z_0uW5E)*

To enhance your experience please pause at this time in reading, and YouTube the following song.

Casting Crowns "No Body"

Why You ever chose me.
Has always been a mystery.
All my life I've been told I belong
At the end of the line
With all the other not-quites
With all the never-get-it-rights
But it turns out they're the ones You were looking for
All this time
'Cause I'm just a nobody
Trying to tell everybody
All about Somebody
Who saved my soul
Ever since You rescued me
You gave my heart a song to sing

I'm living for the world to see
Nobody but Jesus
I'm living for the world to see
Nobody but Jesus
Moses had stage fright
When David brought a rock to a swordfight
You picked twelve outsiders nobody would have chosen
And You changed the world
Well the moral of the story is
Everybody's got a purpose
So when I hear that devil start talking to me saying
"Who do you think you are?"
I say
I'm just a nobody
Trying to tell everybody
All about Somebody
Who saved my soul
Ever since You rescued me
You gave my heart a song to sing
I'm living for the world to see
Nobody but Jesus
I'm living for the world to see
Nobody but Jesus
So let me go down, down, down in history
As another blood-bought faithful member of a family
And if they all forget my name, well that's fine with me
I'm living for the world to see
Nobody but Jesus
So let me go down, down, down in history
(Goin' down in history)
As another blood-bought faithful member
a family
(That's all I ever wanna be)
And if they all forget my name, well that's
fine with me
I'm living for the world to see

Nobody but Jesus
'Cause I'm just a nobody
Trying to tell everybody
All about Somebody
Who saved my soul

Background

Eight-year-old Lizbeth did not say much. She was quiet and watchful. She was always looking for signs that the atmosphere was changing. Her mom suffered from multiple personality disorders and a form of schizophrenia. She had three personalities. Although this diagnosis was not known for many years, Lizbeth always knew her mom suffered from some kind of mental illness. It was normal for Lizbeth to read the physical signs that indicated chaos was about to break out. She tried not to make waves. Her stature was calm, she listened to everything but responded to nothing. She would hear her parents discuss her, "What will ever become of her? Is she dumb?" This would be followed by, "Well at least Pricilla (her older sister) was smart and pretty." Lizbeth just looked out the window at the sky and acted like she didn't hear their curses on her life. She looked to the sky at these moments because she inwardly lifted her pain to God in order to hold back the tears their venomous words invoked. She would not and did not show pain. She dug her heels in and chanted a prayer for the Lord to remove the curse they had just placed on her life. She was not dumb, and she would make something of herself! She prayed, "Use me Lord so my life means something. Don't let me be what they think I am …. A WASTE, in Jesus's name, AMEN." And then her soul found peace. She didn't have to defend herself; she took the hit, and no one knew. Jeremiah

29:11 "For I know the plans I have for you", says the Lord. "They are plans for good and not for disaster, to give you a future and a hope."

Lizbeth knew that she was different from her family. She did not think like them. She had a very different idea of the world. She kept silent because she knew if she expressed her true feelings all hell would break loose. It was better to be silent. Proverbs 10:19: "Silence can help us avoid sinning." Proverbs 11:12: "Silence can gain respect and is deemed wise and intelligent." *Proverbs 17:28* "You are blessed by holding your tongue." Ultimately, refraining from speaking in certain situations means we are practicing self-control. Not only was her family immersed in the mental disorder of their mother, but they were also very prejudiced. They were openly prejudiced against all nationalities, all races, and all religions except for their own. Lizbeth learned how to navigate her world quickly. She would be best pals with her dad because he was lonely because he did not really have a wife. She would comfort her mother when she was crying, hide when she was violent, and be careful when she was nice. When her mom was nice, that's when her mother was collecting ammunition to use to injure the soul of her victim. Lastly, she would keep the house clean to make her mother happy, if that was even possible.

In the past, Lizbeth had learned the hard way, and was easily drawn to her mother when there was a hiatus from the monster, but now she knew better. She used to get sucked into the gifts and affection that would follow one of her mom's episodes, as her dad would call them. She would open her heart, and think maybe Mom would be better now, maybe she did love me. This hope was always extinguished when the raging animal inside her mother would again surface and Mom would use her collected artillery of weaknesses against her prey to annihilate them emotionally. Lizbeth saw the twisted smile on her mother's face one too many times as her mother's victims withered in pain crying. She would take them out at the knees with her viperous tongue. Yes, silence for Lizbeth was the best tactical maneuver. She would never show the enemy her weakness.

This was a lesson her older sister never learned, and because Pricilla (Lizbeth's sister) never adopted the practice of silence, her sister instigated the tumultuous poisons inside their mother and made life even more unbearable. Her sister was supposed to be the smart one. In reality, she was the weak one. She had no inner strength, no gift of observation, and no ability for self-control, no logic. She never read the room. She always said whatever she wanted and in turn always stirred the pot.

Ultimately, Lizbeth's mom played her sister like a fiddle. She could manipulate her to share her deepest secrets, hurts, and desires, and then use all of it against her to emotionally destroy her.

Pricilla was a hot mess. As a child, Lizbeth tried to warn Pricilla. For a while, she even felt sorry for her. She was supposed to be so smart; she was supposed to be the oldest, but Pricilla had been trained that Lizbeth knew nothing and that Pricilla was the smart one. She refused to take any help or advice from her younger and undoubtedly stupid sister. Pricilla saw Lizbeth's silence as an act of stupidity, and weakness. Thus, Pricilla kept falling into the vicious cycle of being manipulated by the moments of niceties from their mother and then being taken out by her ruthless maneuvers to destroy. And destroy they did.

Her mother could usually be found off to herself in a darkened room, with the blinds drawn. If she was not there, she was usually violent and made cruel statements targeted at whoever was in her path. Lizbeth's mother was an equal-opportunity abuser. She was cunning, manipulative, and strategically listened to conversations to gain valuable material to use for verbal destruction. Her mother's ultimate goal was to get the most reaction possible from her victim and cause the most pain. Her victim could be whoever was in her path or whoever fought against her, but the main targets were Lizbeth and Pricilla.

The Day Knowledge Changed Everything

When Lizbeth was 5 years old a Sunday school teacher took a special interest in her. The teacher gave Lizbeth the most valuable gift, not a material gift, but a gift of knowledge. Did this teacher see the hurt behind Lizbeth's eyes? Did Lizbeth's quiet nature give clues of abuse? Was the teacher sent by the Holy Spirit to enlighten Lizbeth? Whatever the reason, one day at Sunday School her teacher took Lizbeth aside and shared with her a more intense version of the salvation story than Lizbeth had ever heard. She told her about God, Jesus, and the Holy Spirit. Her teacher told her that if she had a relationship with them, she could find peace and love. More importantly, the teacher told Lizbeth that if she prayed with her whole heart God would talk to her. Lizbeth thought: What! The girl of quiet silence would have someone to talk to. She could have a confidant. She could share her secrets, her heart, her hurt with SOMEONE who would listen, someone would care. The teacher showed her how to talk to God she said, "Just go somewhere by yourself and talk to Him about everything and anything." She revealed to Lizbeth that God wanted every part of us, the good, the bad, and even the unthinkable. He wanted us to share with Him, be with Him, and walk with Him every day. She told Lizbeth to close her eyes and pretend that Jesus, God, and the Holy Spirit were walking right beside her. Even better, if Lizbeth asked Jesus into her heart, they would be with her all the time. No matter where Lizbeth was, they would be there also. She told Lizbeth she could tell God and Jesus anything, and that they would send Lizbeth help when she most needed it. Lizbeth was mystified, is that true? She asked her teacher why she could not see them. Her teacher replied that Jesus had to go to heaven for a while. He was making a beautiful place for us to go to, but he sent a friend called the Holy Spirit, to be here with all of us. The Holy Spirit guided our path, spoke to us, and was our comforter. Like Casper, Lizbeth thought. The Holy Spirit is a part of Him, so He always knows what we feel and what is going on. She continued by telling Lizbeth that if she concentrated and talked to them, she could feel them. The teacher then placed in Lizbeth's hands two beautiful, folded scripture cards. Lizbeth thought the cards were beautiful. They were engraved with gold writing. One was "The Lord is My Shepherd." Psalm 23 and the other was "The Lord's Prayer." Matthew (6:9–13).

Lizbeth treasured these foldable scripture cards. She went home and placed them on her dresser in the corner of her room and practice these verses daily until soon they would be written on her heart. Lizbeth cannot remember the name or face of this teacher. Maybe she was an angel? In any case, Lizbeth believes they will someday meet again, and her teacher will discover how special those seeds that were sown that day were and how they saved Lizbeth's life but also helped her carry out her destiny.

Home life was always a challenge; over time Mom's episodes became more and more frequent. Lizbeth's dad warned her to never share the dysfunction that was ever-present. In an attempt to scare her into silence, he cautioned her that if anyone found out, the state would take them away and they would have to live with mean strangers. To seal the deal he added, he would never be able to see Lizzie again. Lizzie was her dad's special nickname for her. The circumstance left Lizbeth with only one place she could go for help. She walked and talked with God. She always looked to the sky; she saw Him there. She sang made-up songs about her hurt and asked him to make her strong, to heal her mommy, and to protect her family. She looked at nature to find Him. She saw the sky and how beautiful it was and that it changed every minute. Change she liked the idea that if the sky could change any minute, so could her home situation. God could fix it she thought. She would thank Him in the morning for making her a new sky to look at. She looked at the trees and flowers and saw that each shape of the leaves was different, and the flowers smelled so sweet, and she found peace. "The heavens declare the glory of God; the skies proclaim the work of his hands." Psalm 19.1

To enhance your experience please pause at this time in reading and feel free to YouTube the following song.

Toby Mac, *"Everything"*

I'm captivated, I'll say it
I'm on a whole new intrigue
My space invaded, upgraded
I hear You talking to me
It's in the boom of the thunder, it's in the cool of the rain
And I'll say I don't ever want to get away
Tonight is beautiful
It's got my mind on You
And everywhere I turn is a reminder (reminder, reminder)
I see You in everything, all day
And every beat of my heart keeps reminding me
I see You in every little thing, all day
No matter where I go I know Your love is finding me
I see You in everything
You're all up in everything
My soul's awaken
I'm taken by all the beauty You bring
You got it blarin', I'm starin'
Love watching You do Your thing
There's no mistaking Your style
No mistaking Your touch
I see the grand, I see the subtle of Your love
Lord, I see You in everything, all day
And every beat of my heart keeps reminding me
I see You in every little thing, all day
No matter where I go I know Your love is finding me
It's finding me in everything, all day
And every beat of my heart keeps reminding me
I see You in every little thing, all day
No matter where I go I know Your love is finding me
Tonight is beautiful
It's got my mind on You (got my mind on You)
And everywhere I turn is a reminder (ooh, ooh)
From the sparkle in her eyes to the starlit open skies

You bring my heart to life, fill me with wonder (with wonder, with wonder, with wonder)
I see You in everything, all day (all day!)
And every beat of my heart keeps reminding me
I see You in every little thing, all day (all day!)
No matter where I go I know Your love is finding me
I see You in everything
You're all up in everything
I see You in everything
You're all up in everything
Oh, I can see Your love, Your love in everything
And that's why You'll always be my everything
Yeah, I can see Your love, Your love in everything
And that's why You'll always be my everything

Blissful Summers?

Summers were brutal. Mom hated that Dad was so devoted to his job. She would punish Lizbeth and her sister for the fact that he worked. There were days Lizbeth and Pricilla would be locked outside until their father came home. Those were good days for Lizbeth; she loved being outside. She had a friend next door to play with and she never minded being by herself. Some days when Dad would go to work, Mom would confine Lizbeth and her sister to their rooms. Her mother would say, "If your father loved you, he would come home. He loves his job more than he loves you! He knows you are in your room until he gets home; he is not even thinking about you. WORK! WORK! WORK! That's all he cares about." Then the final blow, she would hit them with words that could not be denied, "He doesn't even care if you eat, so hope your tummies hurt because you are so hungry."

Lizbeth learned to listen at her door, unlock it when her mother would sleep, and slip downstairs to grab a snack. On the way back to her room, she would throw some food into her sister's room. Occasionally she would sneak a call to her dad. She would cry that they had to stay in their rooms until he got home. He would sigh loudly and say, "Lizzie, I have to work, you know this! Where is your mom? Don't get caught being out of your room Lizzie." The consequence of getting caught was hot pepper on the tongue and a ruler to the butt. Not one hit. Multiple hits till mom's anger diminished. Lizzie could sense the stress in her dad's voice, so as not to cause him any more pain, she concealed her own torment and advised him that she had lots to play with in her room, had gotten a snack downstairs and was ok. Daddy's voice sounded proud now, "That's my girl! I will bring home a candy bar from the work vending machine for you…. ok…. Lizzie?" he stopped. "You know I have to work… RIGHT?" "YES, Daddy, I know, it's not your fault, I love you!" Lizzie said and believed it. "Bye Baby" Dad got off the phone with the assurance he needed, he did not think of the home front now until it was time to leave. The question was, did Lizzie get what she needed?

After these extreme episodes, Mom would go out and come home with gifts. Pricilla and Lizbeth would gather around their mother excited to see what Mommy had gotten them. It wasn't so much the gifts that matter it was that Mommy would smile and hug them, and sometimes Mommy would laugh. Mommy did care! She bought presents! But the good mood was always short-lived, soon there would be another episode of anger. Lizbeth would think, Poor mommy is sick again; she must be so sad. She loved her mom, and stored those happy moments with her, in her heart. Eventually, Lizbeth would dread the times when her mom bought these gifts; it came with an obligatory gratefulness and gratitude. Mom required immediate joy and appreciation for each and every gift even if the recipient didn't like the gifts, which were meant to be compensation for the monster's behavior. Lizbeth knew she had to guard her heart against feeling any joy or expectation that maybe her mom's niceness was there to stay. It was too painful for Lizbeth to feel happy only for the rug to be ripped out from under her just moments later when her mother would return to the animal that raged inside of her.

The weekends were great. Dad would always rise early and take Lizzie to the grocery store with him. Then they would take off to a museum or zoo, or fishing, any place but home. The dread was when it was time to go home. In the early years, there were still some good times, as Mom's episodes would come and go. At times, when they would subside, life seemed somewhat normal. During good times, Mom would take Lizbeth and Pricilla out to the 5 and 10 store (kind of like a 5 Below today). As long as they followed Mom's instructions, they might get a milkshake or pretzel and maybe even a candy bar. As Lizbeth got older, she hated candy bars, to this day, she doesn't eat them.

Innocence Stolen

All holidays were rough, Mom's episodes seemed to be more intense during any kind of pending celebrations. Birthdays, Easter, Christmas, and 4th of July (which provided a different kind of fireworks for Lizbeth than the beautiful display that most children enjoyed) all came with low expectations of enjoyment and high alert for episodes of escalation. So, life was full of ups and downs with lots of uncertainties.

Christmas time is a particularly exciting time for 5-year-olds and Lizbeth like most children, had the desire for sugar plums to dance in her head, but her reality was not like that of other children. This Christmas, during one of her mother's "episodes" her mother divulged there would be no Christmas presents, due to the fact that Lizbeth and her sister were bad, and Santa would even be bringing them coal. Her mother sealed this statement with, "Santa thought them so vile; he didn't want to come to their house." Lizbeth decided to test her mother's declaration of no presents, no Christmas, and searched the house to see if there were visible signs of presents.

She knew she shouldn't, but she needed to see if her mom was just being mean or if it was real. It was the day before Christmas, the family tradition was that Santa delivered their favorite gift and filled the stockings. The rest of the gifts were from her parents. Questioning, her mother's verbal threats, Lizbeth set off to see if there were any presents in the house. To her delight she found presents! Lizbeth quickly concealed her discovery and ran to her room. As she jumped and landed on her bed she smiled, relief flooded through her, there would be presents! Mom was just saying mean things again. Forgetting herself, Lizbeth made a fatal mistake. So excited by her discovery and the relief she felt, she decided to share this joy with her sister. This proved to be a huge mistake. Lizbeth knew better than to involve her sister in any secrets, but she did it anyway. What was she thinking? She trusted someone, and not just someone, her sister. As soon as the words were out of her mouth, Lizbeth thought to herself; *Yes, they are right, I am stupid.* But Lizbeth was so excited she couldn't hold it in. Maybe Pricilla will keep her mouth shut? Maybe Pricilla won't tell, tonight was Christmas Eve after all.

Sure enough, Lizbeth's blunder proved catastrophic. In what seemed like seconds Pricilla and their mom got into a battle. Lizbeth knew her goose was going to be cooked, when she heard her mother taunting Pricilla, with that sick twisted joy, that Christmas was indeed canceled. Pricilla just couldn't bask in the reverie that she had special knowledge; Pricilla had to prove Mom wrong. At the top of her lungs, Pricilla screamed loud enough for the neighbors to hear, "That's not true! And then she did it, she threw Lizbeth under the bus and boldly proclaimed Lizbeth's discovery of the presents.

Oh boy, that was it. Her Mom's eyes started to change and the evil voice she would adopt in these moments came out. Rage was on her face, and she turned to Lizbeth,

"You little sneak!

You think you know. I will show you."

Lizbeth stood there in a posture of submission. She lowered her head and tried to look guilty and sorrowful at the same time. She tried to not make eye contact with the evil being in front of her. She knew silence was the answer. When the beast ran out of things to say she would stop. Her mother continued to bombard Lizbeth with insults in an effort to get Lizbeth to react.

"You are worthless!

We never wanted a second child!

We only ever wanted Pricilla!

You were a mistake!

You are a mute and a sneaky little bitch!

I should call the shelter and have them come take you right now!

I already have the paperwork filled out for them to take you.

You are nothing but a runt a little piece of shit that will probably be a midget.

No man will ever want you.

You will be sponging off us forever."

Lizbeth felt the tears well. No, she could not show pain. She could not show that those words hurt her. Those words were too close to her heart. What could she do to calm the beast in her mother? Then she heard His voice; "Submit and Pray!"

So, Lizbeth obeyed; she knelt at her mother's feet, covered her head to avoid being hit on the head, and bowed to her mother. Inside though something different was happening, Lizbeth was not submitting to her mom, she was obeying the voice of God. He is the one who told her what to do. *"Submit and Pray"*. So, pray she did. "Please Lord Calm my mother down. Forgive me for searching the house and being bad. I should have never tried to find the gifts. Please send me help."

Her mother looked down and saw what she thought was a broken child and gained satisfaction that her bombastic rantings did their job. The sick smile was smeared across her face. Whoever her mother was at this moment was different than before. This version of her was cruel and mean and needed to hurt someone. This version would not go away until it felt like it won. It needed to crush the spirit, and Lizbeth knew it. *"Good, you should bow to me, and by the way. THERE IS NO SANTA! And since you were so determined to find your gifts…"*

Her mother left the room and came back with a bag. She opened the bag and threw the unwrapped gifts in front of her little 5-year-old daughter. *"Here are your gifts. MERRY CHRISTMAS. THAT WILL TEACH YOU!"*

Her mother looked for a reaction; Lizbeth was able to give her what she wanted. Lizbeth knew for this monstrous side of her mother to go away, Lizbeth had to cry. She had to show pain, and she had to show that her mom had won the battle. So, she cried. Mom was satisfied, she thought she had crushed the spirit and won, and proceeded to walk out of the room. For Lizbeth, something bigger had happened at that moment. She had gained new strength; she tapped into a power she hadn't felt before, God answered her, and more importantly, HE SPOKE TO HER. Her teacher was right. If you pray with your whole heart God hears you and answers you and… you can hear Him speak. Lizbeth prayed again: "Dear Lord, I know you are listening now… Please heal my mom and take this illness away. Please let us be a normal family. Make her better and make her be a mom that loves and wants me. AMEN"

Lizbeth jumped up and ran to see where her mother had gone. She was expecting God to answer her prayer again, right there and then. She rounded the corner and wrapped her little arms around her mother's legs and said, "Mommy I love you."
Her mother shook her free and looked down at her and said, "Well, I don't love you, how could I love a defect like you?" Lizbeth sat there on the floor while her mother stormed off. The monster was still there. Lizbeth thought, *why didn't God answer me? Do you get only so many answers a day? I will have to try*

again tomorrow. Tomorrow, I will use it as my prayer. God will answer me tomorrow.

Once the sting of her mom's verbal rejection subsided Lizbeth remember, did Mom say there was no Santa? Five-year-old Lizbeth did not believe it. She thought *I will ask Daddy. Mom was just being mean. It cannot be true.* She ran into her father's arms. "Daddy", she sobbed, "Mom said there was no Santa and then threw all my presents at me. Daddy tell me the truth, Is there a Santa?" Her father hugged her and thought for a minute and then replied, "NO honey, there is no Santa."

"What! How can this be true?" Lizbeth cried.

"What, No Santa… Daddy, why did you tell me that?"

"Honey I am sorry, but I never want to Lie to you."

Dad sat on the chair with his face resting in his hands and sighed. That was how Dad sat when he was sad, thought Lizbeth. She loved her Daddy. She did not want him to be sad. "It's ok Daddy, I already knew there was not a Santa, a kid at school told me." She did not look in his eyes or he would have seen she was lying. Daddy picked Lizzie up and pulled her on his lap. She sat there with her head buried in his shoulder, so he could not see her tears.

The next morning Lizzie's dad came into her room very early. He knelt at her bed and said, "Honey, we must play a pretend game today. I need you to pretend yesterday did not happen. You must be surprised by all your presents. Mom wrapped them last night and we put the tree up while you were sleeping. Mom doesn't remember anything that happened. Can you just play the pretend game? If you don't, Mommy will get in a mood again." Lizzie looked at her dad, cupped his face in her little hand, and kissed him."Yes, Daddy!" Lizzie complied. "I can be surprised and pretend yesterday did not happen." Her daddy kissed her and said, "You're my favorite you know?" Lizzie laughed. She did know her daddy liked her best. This made her feel good. She would do anything for him. And so, she did.

It wasn't that hard to pretend that all was ok. Her family's tradition was that the tree was part of their gift. Her dad always put the tree up after the girls went to bed. The reality was, he probably assumed during an episode her mother would tear the tree down if it was put up too soon. Lizbeth always loved coming down and seeing the beautiful tree. Being surprised would be cake. She was happy when she saw the presents wrapped so pretty. She thought, *I don't know which are which; I can be surprised. I only saw them for a second, so I **will** be surprised.* With each package she opened, she laughed and said thank you right away so as not to make her mother get mad. The plan was working until… Pricilla.

Ooooh NOOOO, she didn't. Pricilla opened her 3rd present and did not like it. "Oh, I don't like this one! Can it be taken back?", bellowed Pricilla. It felt purposeful. Did Pricilla want to ruin Christmas? Did she want their mom to get in another mood? Maybe she did, but one thing was for sure, if you wanted to set their mother off, ungratefulness was a sure trigger. Lizbeth looked into her mom's eyes to see the reaction. Nothing? *Ok! ok, maybe it will be ok*, Lizzie thought.

Her mother replied, "That's ok, put it aside, but open this one. I know it will be your favorite. I went to 3 stores to find it and I got it in the color you love." *Wow! Saved, Thank you Lord,* Lizbeth thought. Bullet dodged.

Lizbeth continued opening gifts, she kept smiling and kept acting surprised. Pricilla took her next gift from their mother. "That's not the one I wanted." "This will have to go back too", barked Pricilla.

Are you kidding me? Lizbeth thought. *And I am the stupid one? Why can't she just keep her mouth shut? How can she not know what sets off Mom's moods? I hate Pricilla.*

Lizbeth looked at her mom and she opened her next gift quickly, in order to compensate for her sister's blunder, Lizbeth said, "Oh Mommy, I love this! How did you know I wanted it? This is my favorite gift." Nothing. No reaction. Mom was glaring at Pricilla now. "Oh, Mommy it is beautiful," Lizbeth said with more joy to divert the damage done by Pricilla's rejection of not 1 but 2 gifts. Her mother looked at her with a half-smile, somewhat amused. But her eyes were focused on Pricilla who was oblivious to what she had just done. Then Lizbeth saw it, The Eyes. Rage came, and Christmas was over. Mom threw the gifts across the room and down came the tree. Ornaments and lights went flying, Dad sat on the sofa with his face in his hands and Pricilla and Lizbeth scattered for cover. Pricilla got it good this time. This time Lizbeth didn't feel sorry for her. Afterward, Lizzie helped Dad clean up the mess while Mom slept.

Day At the Beach

Lizbeth had no idea how important her knowledge of God would be until that day she really cried for help. The day started out well. Her family had decided to go down the shore for the day. Lizbeth was 7. They piled into the car with hopes of being at the beach in 3 hours. After about an hour, the mood started to shift in her mom. She was becoming antsy, and easily provoked. A discussion broke out with her dad and now the intensity of mom's mood was escalating. Lizzie put her little hand on her father's shoulder. She gave him a warning look that it was time to retreat. He eyed Lizzie in the rearview mirror, caught the prompt, and silenced himself. Lizzie exhaled hoping her mother would de-escalate, but no, Pricilla was there, and she would finish the job.

As mom was left disappointed in Dad's lack of response, she needed something to keep her fires from extinguishing; she wanted a fight. It was almost like their mom liked how it felt to be out of control, the feeling of being enraged. Did it make her feel powerful? Did it make her feel in control? Their mom liked when things went her way that was for sure, and she hated to lose, so mom turned to Pricilla. Mom knew Pricilla could be manipulated, so she ordered Pricilla to put sunscreen on. They were still 2 hours away from the beach. There was no need for such a request. Mom was looking for a reason to explode and Pricilla was the girl to provide it. So it began:

"Pricilla start putting the sunscreen on," their mom barked. "NO, it will make me sticky in the car", Pricilla, sassed back.

Lizbeth tried to intervene. She whispered to Pricilla, "Just look like you are putting it on to make her happy. You don't have to actually put it on yet. Just pretend. " Lizbeth started to put some lotion on her arm for moral support. "NO!", Pricilla yelled at Lizbeth, "I am not going to pretend to put it on to make her happy. I don't care if she flips like a Psycho. I AM NOT DOING IT!"

Then Lizbeth saw it, her mom had one blue and one brown eye, and when in good spirits her blue eye was light, clear, and sparkled like a clear lake with the sky reflected in it, her brown eye was warm and a beautiful cocoa color. However, when their mom's mood turned, so did her eyes change also. It was a sign that it was time to hide. But where? Where can you hide in the car? It was too late, mom turned around from the front seat with a look to kill. Her brown eye had clouded over and was cold and dark, the blue eye had turned to a gray murky color. Here came the rage.

"I SAID, PUT THE SUNSCREEN ON NOW!" their mom reverberated. "NO, I'm not gonna! You're crazy, I am in the car. No one is going to get burnt." screamed Pricilla. Pricilla had said the two tabu words, Psycho, and Crazy. These words were enough to launch a full fledge episode. And so, they did. *"DO IT NOW!"* their mother screamed in that evil voice that came on during these times. Then the swinging of hands to the back seat began. Their mom was now reaching for a weapon that could be used as a paddle. She wouldn't stop now until the rage that had been ignited ran its course. This was going to be bad. Their dad pulled over, mistake if only he had kept driving. Now it was a barrage of hair-pulling, screaming, spitting, and biting. Two savages going at it while the ongoing cars that passed by slowed to look at the show. This was all over a battle of wills. Lizbeth hated Pricilla at that moment. Why couldn't she just comply? Why not just start to put the sunscreen on until their mom's attention was redirected? Couldn't Pricilla keep the peace? Was all this worth it? Maybe to Pricilla, it was. She was going to be her own person and fight back. She was not going to pretend to be controlled. For Lizbeth, it was easier. She could submit without submitting. She could comply without really complying.

The result was that after crossing over the Walt Whitman Bridge from Pennsylvania to NJ, their mother got out of the car and decided she was going to walk home. What would have been an hour ride home became a 5-hour event while they tried to get their mom back into the car. This meant hours upon hours of their dad following behind her in the car. Dad never drove off during these events for fear that something might happen to their mom. After multiple events like this, Lizbeth wondered if maybe it would be ok if something happened to her mom. Her mother could not be happy, and she made the family miserable. Maybe it would be ok. These thoughts would always lead to a feeling of guilt; Lizbeth would feel like a horrible person. How could she think something so horrible? She was a bad person.

Dad always sent Lizzie out to the street at times like this, and this time was no different. Lizzie was sent to negotiate, coax, lure, whatever it would take to get their mom back into the car. At dusk, probably due to sheer exhaustion, Mom finally decided it was time to get back in the car. She did not speak a word; her feet were blistered and bleeding from wearing improper shoes for such an undertaking. Her skin was burned from being in the hot sun, ironically without sunscreen. They were all hungry, but no one dared to ask Dad to stop for food, even Pricilla for fear that stopping would start the walkabout once more.

That evening was peaceful and the next day as well. Their mother slept, exhausted from the previous days' events, but all that sleep only gave her vigor. The following day, Mom started the day like a snake. Lizbeth awoke with the sound of pots and pans being clanged together while Mom chanted in a sing-song evil laughter, striking pots and pans together in an attempt to wake everyone from their peaceful slumber.

"Get up! Get up! ha-ha ha-ha.

Today is the day you are all gonna DIE."

Lizbeth sprung to her feet, still half groggy from dreaming. She went running from her room, but her mother stopped her in the doorway.

31

"Where are you going? Looking for your DADDY? He can't help you! Today is the day you are gonna die!"

Mom's fury was worse than normal; she looked evil. The rage in her mother was at DEFCON 4, system overload. The next thing Lizbeth knew her mother had thrusted the heel of her hand against Lizbeth's tiny chest causing Lizbeth to hit the side of the bed. As her mother continued to advance, she grabbed a wooden shoe with one hand and Lizbeth's arm with the other. Lizbeth knew better than to fight the beast. Her mother threw her on the bed onto her stomach and started the tirade of hits to Lizbeth's bottom. Lizbeth clenched her teeth as tears flowed down her little face. She wheezed after each hit; she knew from Pricilla that if you fought back, you got more hits, so she laid there and counted inside her head. 1,2,3,4,5,6……. Then they stopped. Was it over? Had the beast gotten tired? Lizbeth tried to hold back the sobs; she knew that crying would only reignite the beast. Her little legs were shaking, and her butt felt numb, her back hurt too, she was warm, she had wet the bed. In sheer exhaustion her mother dropped the wooden clog on the floor and slammed the door shut.

Lizbeth started to cry, not just any cry, the hyperventilating type of cry when you are in sheer panic. She did not know where her dad was, he was silent. Did her mother kill him? Lizbeth could smell a strong odor now in the house. She was not sure what it was, but it didn't smell good. Her mother had put the stove on and was filling

the house with gas. She could hear her mother breathing outside her door. She was speaking in a different voice now. An evil villainous voice, she was whispering through the door to taunt Lizbeth.
"I killed your Daddy, now you have no one.

Now it is your turn. I will rid the world of you. I am gonna light a match and poof the whole house will go up in flames!" Her mother screamed like an unnatural being. Then an ungodly screech came through the door, "You will burn alive. Hahahahahahaha".

Lizbeth could not feel her legs, and her arms were shaking, she was finding it hard to breathe. Was her dad dead? Did her mother kill him? Then she saw them, right on her dresser were the two foldable cards her teacher had given her. Lizbeth grabbed them in her hand and then hid herself in the corner of her room. She closed her eyes and recited: "The Lord is my shepherd; I shall not want. He maketh me to lie down in green pastures: he leadeth me beside the still waters. He restoreth my soul: he leadeth me in the paths of righteousness for his name's sake Yea, though I walk through the valley of the shadow of death, I will fear no evil: for thou art with me; thy rod and thy staff they comfort me. Thou preparest a table before me in the presence of mine enemies: thou anointest my head with oil; my cup runneth over. Surely goodness and mercy shall follow me all the days of my life: and I will dwell in the house of the Lord forever." Psalm 23
Again, and again and again she recited.

Then she opened the other card and closed her eyes and prayed: "Our Father, which art in heaven, Hallowed be thy Name. Thy Kingdom comes. Thy will be done on earth as it is in heaven. Give us this day our daily bread. And forgive us our trespasses, as we forgive them that trespass against us. And lead us not into temptation but deliver us from evil. For thine is the kingdom, The power, and the glory, Forever and ever."

She recited the second card again, and again and again. Then she prayed: "Dear Lord. I love you. Save me from my mom. I am yours."

And there it was, just like her teacher had said, God spoke, "I am here. I see you. You will be ok, do not fear, you have a special job to do for me. Wait and see. You will be ok. I will never leave you. I will protect you."

Lizbeth woke. She had fallen asleep on her bed; she was clueless as to how much time had passed, but things were quiet. She had a hard time moving, her butt really hurt and so did her back. She got up and surveyed the damage in the mirror, her back had several large welts and was already starting to bruise, her butt...... welted, bruised, and bleeding. "OUCH", she wanted to lie down on her bed and cry, but she needed to see where Daddy was. Where was he? He didn't come to help! In the past, he would be there and say, "Lizbeth is so tiny, STOP, you are going to break something." This time he didn't come. Did the beast kill him? She cautiously went to the door

34

and opened it; her mom was nowhere in sight. She found her dad, sitting downstairs in the chair, hopelessly resting his face in his hands. She looked at him and all she could feel was "My poor Daddy is sad." Later, as she got older and reflected on this event, Lizbeth asked, why didn't my dad try to save me? Why didn't he try to protect me? But on that day, all she felt was my poor Daddy is sad. Daddy never asked her how she was, even though her gait made it clear that she was not ok. The episode was over, Mom was sleeping. Dad took Lizbeth and Pricilla out for ice cream, this was a small constellation prize, but Lizbeth accepted that it was the best that Daddy could offer. It took about a week before Lizbeth could ride her bike again. The next trash day, Lizbeth snuck the wooden shoes into the trash can; they were never seen again.

All Lizbeth focused on was she had felt calm when God answered her. He showed up! Just like her teacher said He would. Again, God showed up when she needed Him the most. He was there. She did not understand it at that moment, but now she believes that God did not just save her, He changed her. She not only received salvation that day, but he blanketed her with a forcefield of protection. He opened her eyes to see the truth, and He gave her hope for the future. He continually told her that things will be different for her. He told her she would be here in the future. He told her He had a job for her to do. She was special to Him. God wanted her to do something. She would do anything for Him.

From that day on, no matter how hard things got or what her eyes saw, her mind and soul became stronger in Him, and she called on Him eagerly. He did not allow her to become hardened, or damaged. She felt His presence around her. When her mother would say hurtful things, He would whisper in her head, "No, that is not true! You are loved by me. I chose you. You are mine." And so, she was. God told her that she belonged to Him, and she believed Him. She loved Him. She would do anything for Him.1 John 3:1 "God's love got you is lavish. "See what great love the Father has lavished on us, that we should be called children of God!"

Chis Tomlin, "I Will Follow"

Where You go, I'll go
Where You stay, I'll stay
When You move, I'll move
I will follow
All Your ways are good
All Your ways are sure
I will trust in You alone
Higher than my side
High above my life
I will trust in You alone
Where You go, I'll go
Where You stay, I'll stay
When You move, I'll move
I will follow You
Who You love, I'll love
How You serve I'll serve
If this life I lose, I will follow You
I will follow You

Light unto the world
Light unto my life
I will live for You alone
You're the one I seek
Knowing I will find
All I need in You alone, in You alone
Where You go, I'll go
Where You stay, I'll stay
When You move, I'll move
I will follow You
Who You love, I'll love
How You serve I'll serve
If this life I lose, I will follow You
I will follow You, yeah
In You there's life everlasting
In You there's freedom for my soul
In You there's joy, unending joy
And I will follow
Where You go, I'll go
Where You stay, I'll stay
When You move, I'll move
I will follow
Who You love, I'll love
How You serve I'll serve
If this life I lose, I will follow
Where You go, I'll go
Where You stay, I'll stay
When You move, I'll move
I will follow You
Who You love, I'll love
How You serve I'll serve
If this life I lose, I will follow You, yeah
I will follow You, yeah
I will follow You, yeah
I will follow You, yea

Relatives No More

The one family member Lizzie got to see was her mom's sister, Aunt Ginny. Aunt Ginny called her Lizzie too, and Lizzie saw her as a mom. Aunt Ginny did not know all that was going on, but she had a way of calming Lizbeth's mom. Here and there Aunt Ginny would make statements that made Lizzie think she knew their secret. Lizzie learned from her aunt that her mom had been an emotional girl growing up. Emotional? Hmmmm Lizzie thought they have no idea. Aunt Ginny always offered for Pricilla and Lizzie to sleep over at her house. Lizzie would always jump at the opportunity, but Pricilla did not get along with Aunt Ginny's son, so she never did. Aunt Ginny made Lizzie laugh; sometimes Lizzie wished Aunt Ginny would be her mom. Over and over Aunt Ginny would whisper to Lizzie that she was her favorite; that meant the world to Lizzie. Her Aunt also enjoyed the outdoors which was Lizzie's haven. Anything outside meant she could be at peace. So, when the families got together, this was a piece of heaven for Lizzie. Also, her aunt had really cool snacks at her house.

On occasion, both families would go on vacation together, until the incident on that fatal summer trip. Lizbeth was seven. They had gone camping with her aunt. Her Aunt had a camper, and it was a cool one, the kind you could drive. When they got to the campground there was a lake, bikes, a petting zoo, and playground equipment, best of all, everything was outside. This was going to be the best vacation ever. Lizzie could retreat from her mom, hang with her Aunt Ginny, and be outside. Life was good.

On the second day of the trip, Lizzie got up early and wanted to take a walk. She was told to stay near the trailer, but she could wander a little and collect nature stuff. Lizzie took the time to spread a blanket in the early sun and bask in the warmth. She looked to the sky and thanked God for how beautiful it was again. She thanked Him for the great vacation and being able to camp. Mom hadn't been so bad lately, so she thanked Him for making her a little better, but could He please make her all the way better?

She almost fell back to sleep when she was startled by yelling coming from the trailer. It was morning so everything had been quiet. The only noise was the peaceful sound of doves making their coo, a woodpecker rat-tat-tatting on some trees, and other birds chirping. It was like paradise until Lizzie's uncle decided that while he was blanketed by the presence of Lizzie's parents, he would tell Aunt Ginny that he had cheated on her. People were coming out of their trailers looking around and watching the morning entertainment. There was crying, cursing, and objects flying. The next thing Lizzie knew, her dad was packing up the car. Mom was crying and the Vacation was over.

Lizbeth thought the news was more devastating for her mom than for her aunt. Something broke in Lizbeth's mom with that news. To her, all men were now cheaters; the unfaithfulness the uncle had afforded to the aunt was being placed upon Lizzie's father as well. Lizbeth did not understand fully what cheating meant, so her mother told her in a very descriptive and repulsive manner about unfaithfulness. That was Lizbeth's first class in sex education. Yuck. Lizbeth was seven.

There were no more vacations, no more aunt, and no more family outings. Lizbeth's mom spiraled into paranoia. There were scenes of Mom throwing all of Dad's things out the window, locking him out of the house, trying to stab him with a knife, hitting him, and telling him to leave. Yet he stayed. He taught Lizzie how to cook and take care of the house. He would wake her in the wee hours of the morning and ask her to go talk to her mother whom he had been ministering to all night. He would tell Lizzie he had to get some sleep-in order to go to work in the morning. Lizzie dutifully would roll out of bed and go down to a pitch-dark room and find her mother half naked crying with mucus streaming from her nose to her leg. Trying not to gag, she would wipe her mother's nose and get a cold cloth for her head. She would tell her mom how much she loved her and wanted her to feel better. Her mother would look at her, spread her legs, and masturbate right in front of Lizbeth. She told Lizbeth that she did not need a man in her life. Men were no good. If Lizbeth thought her dad was any different, she was wrong. He could cheat just as easily. Lizbeth was seven.

To enhance your experience please pause at this time in reading and feel free to YouTube the following song.

Lauren Daigle, "<u>Rescue</u>"

You are not hidden
There's never been a moment
You were forgotten
You are not hopeless
Though you have been broken
Your innocence stolen
I hear you whisper underneath your breath
I hear your SOS, your SOS
I will send out an army to find you
In the middle of the darkest night
It's true, I will rescue you
There is no distance
That cannot be covered
Over and over
You're not defenseless
I'll be your shelter
I'll be your armor
I hear you whisper underneath your breath
I hear your SOS, your SOS
I will send out an army to find you
In the middle of the darkest night
It's true, I will rescue you
I will never stop marching to reach you
In the middle of the hardest fight
It's true, I will rescue you
I hear the whisper underneath your breath
I hear you whisper, you have nothing left
I will send out an army to find you
In the middle of the darkest night

It's true, I will rescue you
I will never stop marching to reach you
In the middle of the hardest fight
It's true, I will rescue you
Oh, I will rescue you

Fresh Start

Around this time Lizzie fully formed her allegiance to her father. She secretly sided with her father. He had not been unfaithful, her uncle had. Her father was there and didn't leave. Lizzie became her father's confidant, the homemaker, and the cook. She made sure that she did whatever made her dad happy because she wanted him to have a reason to stay. She liked what shows he liked, what sports he liked, and whatever he liked doing she liked doing. He would talk to her like she was an adult, discuss finances, life issues, and his burdens. Yes, Lizzie became a little adult by the time she was 9.

Dad was doing well at work; he felt that maybe moving to a bigger home would give everyone a fresh start. He built the dream house their mother always wanted, hoping this would bring her happiness. So, they moved a half hour away to the city of Lansdale. Their neighborhood was sandwiched between 3 farms and life was grand for a while. It was a grandiose 3000 square foot home, colonial brick front house with a covered front porch; it looked like it belonged in Williamsburg, Va.

The house was in a neighborhood where the girls could ride bikes, and play outside with friends, and commune with nature. There were three local farms that had cows, chickens, goats, and even homemade ice cream. It was like Lizbeth died and went to heaven. On days her mom locked her out of the house Lizbeth had all the entertainment she could ask for. Dad would whistle when he got home from work so as long as she was in earshot of his whistle, she was free. Free from the moods, free from the nasty comments, free to be whatever you wanted to be. On good days, mom wouldn't lock the door, so you could come home and grab some food or even take a nap if you were tired. As hard as she played, she sometimes liked to relax and take a nap.

Lizbeth had a problem. She was nine and she sucked her thumb. She never did it in public, but if she was alone in her room or when she slept, she would find comfort sucking her thumb. Mom hated it and would call her a baby. Dad would say, "She will stop when she is ready." Lizzie didn't know why she still sucked her thumb, she had many strep throat infections because of it, but for whatever reason, it made her feel safe. She also thought it tasted good.

By now, Pricilla and Lizbeth did not get along very well. Pricilla was always causing turmoil in the house. She always knew how to get their mother to explode, and Lizbeth was done with it. Pricilla got all the attention, but really who needed that kind of attention? Lizbeth thought *Pricilla can have it*. Pricilla would start her shenanigans and Lizbeth would just slip out of sight. *Pricilla can do her thing*, Lizbeth thought. *Maybe Mom and Pricilla will kill each other*. Lizbeth really didn't want anything bad to happen to them, but she was tired of all the fighting. In fact, Lizbeth thought maybe their mom would not be that bad if Pricilla wasn't always pushing her buttons. Anyway, Lizbeth had freedom, so she tried to just forget about the violence that Pricilla and her mother engaged in. The only time Lizbeth got involved at this point was if their mother was picking on their dad. She would take a bullet for him or in this case a knife for him. That was usually the thing mom would threaten them with these days.

Pricilla was not as content. She had started to notice the allegiance Lizbeth had with their dad. She was jealous. By now, it was clear that Lizbeth was her dad's favorite. She did everything with him and the only time he smiled or laughed was when Lizbeth was around. None of it was purposeful, but sometimes they would stop talking when Pricilla entered the room. It was not personal, but Pricilla had a mouth, which always caused their mom to escalate. Pricilla was self-centered and Dad needed someone selfless. Lizbeth's love for her dad made her the perfect candidate to be his geisha, not in an unthinkable way, but certainly in the way she made him feel. The earth stopped when Dad got home. She only did things that he wanted to do. Conversely, Pricilla was mean-spirited and disrupted any peace Lizbeth and Dad could find when she was around.

The relationship that Lizbeth and their dad had infuriated Pricilla and she started to look for ways to get Lizbeth in trouble. If something broke, Pricilla would blame it on Lizbeth. When their mother got involved, Lizbeth would take the hit and remain silent. It was easier to get hit and do chores than to escalate her mother's furry. Lizbeth certainly was not going to engage in a fight with Pricilla either. Pricilla stood at least 3 feet taller than Lizbeth. Lizbeth was in 4th grade at this point and weighed a whopping 46 pounds, her ideal weight should have been 73 pounds. The downside of Lizbeth's suppression of emotions due to her mother's episodes was that Lizbeth had become anorexic. She was no match for Pricilla who towered over her. It was as if the girls were from two different gene pools. Lizbeth had tiny midget genes and Pricilla had Amazon/Viking genes. However, Lizbeth was fast, she could outrun even the fastest boy at school. Pricilla was ruthless, so when she tried to engage in sibling annihilation, Lizbeth's saving grace was her speed and wit to foil Pricilla's pursuit. Pricilla saw Lizbeth as her adversary, not her sister, not her co-victim of this dysfunctional world. She did not like the confidence that Lizbeth projected, nor that Lizbeth acted like the oldest. Most of all she did not like that Lizbeth had the attention of their father.

So, Pricilla set a plan into action. Lizbeth had been playing outside since dawn, by mid-afternoon she was tired. She retreated to her room to chill for a while, as she got sleepy and started to doze that is when her thumb would slip into her mouth. Pricilla knew Lizbeth sucked her thumb, and that it was a secret Lizbeth would want to be taken to the grave. She knew Lizbeth was very careful not to give any telltale signs of this practice in public. This set the stage for Pricilla's attempt to not just humiliate her sister, but put her in her place, under Pricilla's thumb. It was the perfect storm.

Pricilla waited just long enough for Lizbeth to fall asleep. She then executed her plan of humiliation and invited 3 kids, notorious for gossip, into the house and upstairs where Lizbeth lay sleeping with her thumb in tow. Friends were never invited inside because mom did not like company, plus they could never be sure what condition their mother's mental state would be, but Pricilla rolled the dice and hope for a duce. She was already tasting the sweet taste of victory. She knew how to take her sister down and was prepared to play her hand. Pricilla brought the renegades upstairs and stopped in front of Lizbeth's room. There lay Lizbeth, sound asleep with thumb in mouth. Lizbeth awoke with a screeching of laughter as she was mocked and teased for being a thumb sucker. Lizbeth's eyes opened wide as she saw a very familiar smirk on her sister's face. Where had she seen it before? It was the same smirk her mother wore many times. Pricilla was full of joy as everyone laughed and teased Lizbeth for being a baby, Pricilla had won. She embarrassed her sister to tears.

It was rare for her family to sit together and talk. One day, Lizbeth decided to experiment with some of her theories on the need for her silence. As her family was having a racially discriminating conversation, she boldly said, I think someday I could see myself adopting a black child. Lizbeth expressed her feelings with joy and pride. She felt empowered for the first time. She understood life better than they did. She saw God's heart; she felt his love for all people. She had something valuable to say, and she said it. For one second, she believed that maybe she could break down her family's shallow views. She felt free and full of vigor, but the diatribe that followed as her family attempted to correct what they considered her erroneous thinking wasn't worth it.

Lizbeth became silent again. Her parents saw her silence as repentance, dumb Lizbeth had to be corrected for her dumb little ideas. It was at that moment that Lizbeth knew the thoughts she had were not her thoughts, but that of God. He was revealing to her something that she would do. She looked to the sky as she often did determine to see God's plan to fruition. Although she would never express it again to her family, she knew He had revealed to her a glimpse of her future. Lizbeth knew that the Lord was leading her on a different path than her family. He had set her apart for some reason. She was going to do things differently and she knew it. Later the Lord would confirm that this feeling she had was indeed right. He wanted her to do something, but did she have to be embarrassed like that? Did she always have to feel like such an outsider? Romans 8:28 "And we know that for those who love God, all things work together for good. For those who are called according to His purpose."

To enhance your experience please pause at this time in reading and feel free to YouTube the following song.

Mathew West, "*Truth Be Told*"

Lie number one you're supposed to have it all together
And when they ask how you're doing
Just smile and tell them, "Never better"
Lie number 2 everybody's life is perfect except yours
So keep your messes and your wounds
And your secrets safe with you behind closed doors
Truth be told
The truth is rarely told, now
I say I'm fine, yeah I'm fine oh I'm fine, hey I'm fine but I'm not
I'm broken
And when it's out of control I say it's under control but it's not
And you know it
I don't know why it's so hard to admit it
When being honest is the only way to fix it
There's no failure, no fall
There's no sin you don't already know
So let the truth be told
There's a sign on the door, says, "Come as you are" but I doubt it
'Cause if we lived like it was true, every Sunday morning pew would
be crowded
But didn't you say the church should look more like a hospital
A safe place for the sick, the sinner and the scarred and the
prodigals
Like me
Well truth be told
The truth is rarely told

Oh am I the only one who says
I'm fine, yeah I'm fine oh I'm fine, hey I'm fine but I'm not
I'm broken
And when it's out of control I say it's under control but it's not
And you know it
I don't know why it's so hard to admit it
When being honest is the only way to fix it
There's no failure, no fall
There's no sin you don't already know
So let the truth be told
Can I really stand here unashamed
Knowin' that you love for me won't change?
Oh God if that's really true
Then let the truth be told
I say I'm fine, yeah I'm fine oh I'm fine, hey I'm fine but I'm not
I'm broken
And when it's out of control I say it's under control but it's not
And you know it
I don't know why it's so hard to admit it
When being honest is the only way to fix it
There's no failure, no fall
There's no sin you don't already know
Yeah I know
There's no failure, no fall
There's no sin you don't already know
So let the truth be told

13 - Not for the Faint Hearted

Sometime between the age of 9 and 13, Lizbeth felt more in control, so her anorexia began to wane. She was able to divorce her mother's episodes and cast them out of her mind more easily even though the turmoil in the house had reached an all-time high. Her dad kept telling her that her mother was going through menopause and that was why mom's emotional stability had declined even further. The episodes that had been limited to celebratory events, were now an almost daily occurrence. This was easier, knowing this was the norm, than living with the unexpected. Knowing what to expect with no surprises made the tension subside, making it easier to deal with.

The only respite Lizbeth had now, was the time she was at school. She no longer looked forward to days off or snow days or the dreaded summer vacation. Anytime school was in session it meant she was not home with her mother. In reality, her mother's disorder had hit a pinnacle. She should have been hospitalized. Company never crossed the family threshold; friends were never allowed to come to hang out. Lizbeth struggle for a life of normalcy, so she decided to test the waters and invited a friend to the house to work on a project for school. This act proved to be enlightening.

In a moment of sheer denial, Lizbeth asked her dad if a new friend could come home to work on a school project. This was like social suicide, interesting enough suicidal was the word for age thirteen. The moment her friend entered the house, Lizbeth's mother scrutinized the girl, eyeing her friend from head to toe, with a look of disgust on her face. Her mother did not say hello nor address the friend with any normal salutations. Seeing the heightened agitation in her mother, Lizbeth carted her friend up to her room to work on a project. She ran back downstairs, with the premise to get a few snacks, and submitted to her mother in order to calm the waters. "Sorry Mommy, she won't be here long. We just have a project for school."

Lizbeth's mom said nothing, she didn't have to, Lizbeth looked at her mother's face and she saw "THE EYES", Mom's unspoken telltale sign, it was time to run. At 13, Lizbeth did not feel that panicked anymore over the 'EYES". Her mother had already made a spectacle of herself when she offered no greets to her friend. Deep down, Lizbeth almost wanted her to make a scene. She wanted the monster to come out in front of her friend. Then someone would know, she would be innocent of telling their secret. *Go Ahead!* She thought *DO IT, DO IT! Show how you really are. Then maybe we can get help.*

Her mom didn't disappoint but it was not the full fledge monster, Lizbeth had anticipated. It was like Mom was holding back. Interesting, could Mom control the monster inside of her? Was being like this her choice? That was the first time Lizbeth ever questioned whether her mom could choose to be different. This possibility was scarier than the EYES itself. This thought made things unbearable. It was one thing if someone couldn't help it. It was another if they could.

As if her mother was reading Lizbeth's thought she engaged half throttle. "Why did you bring this whore to the house. Look at her she is sheer trash. Get her out of here now. "Fortunately? Lizbeth wasn't so sure, but her friend was tucked away in her room and didn't hear a thing. Her mother's outburst wouldn't have been enough to help them anyway. It would have only been enough to say her mother was rude. But the realization of her mom having self-control resonated in Lizbeth's mind and heart. Ouch... Mom can control herself if she wants to. She chooses to be this way. Dad who usually did nothing but sit in a chair with his face in his hands, actually came in as the savior. What? Is this like Friday the 13th? The world had shifted, the norms Lizbeth had come to count on changed and so did her perspective on their family. Dad suggested that he take Lizbeth and her friend to Roy Rodgers for dinner, and they could finish their project there. Score.... Roy Rogers was like an upscale Mcdonalds', but they only went there as a treat. She would take it as a win. Even Mom's face showed an expression of being pleased. Dad told Mom he would bring her a meal back. It was not refused, and it seemed to calm the beast.

After that, Lizbeth's parents took her out of public school and placed her in an academic prep school. The school was over 30 minutes from her home, so the excuse for no visitor from school was justified with distance. Lizbeth wondered if the close call that transpired with her friend was a contributing factor. After the debacle, Lizbeth's dad warned her to never bring anyone to the house again. It was too risky. He looked into Lizbeth's eyes and saw something different for the first time. He saw compliance, not submission. He no longer saw fear; he saw fear replaced by knowledge.

This knowledge for Lizbeth shifted the pendulum. The metronome was off kilter, it was no longer a constant beat. If mom could control herself, what did that mean? Did she want to be like this? Did she want to be a bad mother? The things she said...... she really meant? What about Dad? Sad Dad. All these times she felt sorry for him while he sat there in a chair with his hands on his face doing nothing to stop her. But this time, he protected. This time he was the savior. Why? Did he do it for Lizbeth? Himself? Mom? Her friend? It was too much to consider. Was there some kind of sick need for them to live this way? Did Dad vow them to secrecy for their protection or was it a way to not get help? System overload, Lizbeth chose to think about it later.

Interestingly she did not pray about it or go to God with it. She didn't even think about Him at this moment. She was calm but full of thoughts. She would look for the answers another day. Lizbeth didn't realize that her relationship with God was proportional to her level of strength, peace, and resolve. Had she known this, she surely would not have put Him on the shelf again. John 1:3 "Grace, mercy and peace will be with us, from God the Father and Jesus". Psalm 46:1-3 "God is our refuge and strength ever-present help in trouble.

Both Pricilla and Lizbeth now attended a renowned prep school. Ironically an entrance exam was given before they were accepted. Lizbeth scored significantly higher than Pricilla did. Hmm…The first year was hard academically. It was a K-12 school and those students that had attended in lower grades were so far ahead academically. On day one of Spanish class the teacher came in and spoke nothing but Spanish. The homework was in Spanish, the instruction was in Spanish. The first semester proved to Lizbeth that she was stupid. It was hard, but over time Lizbeth caught up and life at school at least was good.

Adolescents hit hard for Pricilla. It came in like a tsunami. Lizbeth did feel bad for her, but at the same time, like everything else, she felt that Pricilla had brought it on herself. Pricilla was a consumer of greasy junk food with a side of chocolate. Anything, good for her, she hated. She would inhale bags of greasy chips, chocolate tasty-cake cupcakes, and candy. These foods only exacerbated her acne issues. Although by thirteen Lizbeth was coming out of the anorexia phase, she did learn some really healthy eating habits from it. She learned what to eat that gave not only little consequence to weight gain, but foods that were good for the skin. If Lizbeth was hungry, she ate the entire head of lettuce, or the entire stalk of celery, cut up carrots and apples were always a tummy filler, yet would not add meat to the bones, Consequently, Lizbeth suffered from only an occasional pimple, while Pricilla was covered, her face, back, shoulders, arms and chest were one massive dermatological nightmare. This did not help Pricilla's disposition to say the least, nor did the freakish pimple-less Lizbeth, help with Pricilla's jealousy.

Lizbeth in essence was the antithesis of her sister, not only in stature and skin tone, but also in personality. Lizbeth stood about 4'11 and weighed a whopping 83 pounds. She had long curly sun kissed brown hair and her skin tone was olive, so she would tan easily. She had basically shake-and-go hair after a shower, long eyelashes, with blue eyes. Her demeanor was calm, quiet, and at least outwardly submissive. Conversely, Pricilla was 5'8, not heavy, but not thin either, fair-skinned, which burned to a crisp in summers, with mid-length dirty blonde hair that was poker straight and would not take a curl. Her demeanor was hot-headed, intolerant, and vocal. To top it off, Pricilla had allergies. She was allergic to everything. Conveniently, she also used allergies to avoid doing any kind of chores around the house. She could not do any yard work… "Oh No, My Allergies", she could not dust "Oh No my allergies!" She could not clean the bathrooms because the smell of cleaner affected her allergies. Yada yada yada. So basically, Priscilla was useless. If she tried to cook anything, she would burn whatever she prepared. Lizbeth often wondered if she acted helpless on purpose or was it if a clever tactical strategy to get out of doing any work. As they both got older, Lizbeth saw Pricilla as a mini version of their mother. A mini mom… Scary.

Normalcy settled in for a while. Lizbeth got used to Mom's constant moods, she balanced school and home ok and she felt all was ok. She spent little time with God. Oh, maybe a quick prayer here and there, but she had definitely put him on that proverbial shelf. She felt she was able to handle things on her own now. Dad was happy with her, coming home from work with dinner ready, the house cleaned, and Lizbeth there to greet him by updating him on the status of the home front, yes Lizbeth was a well-oiled machine and it worked for him. She was managing a household and doing well at it she thought. Lizbeth had more of herself than God in her life. She felt strong, powerful, and accomplished for once in her life. She did not realize how debilitating life could feel without the protection and comfort the Holy Spirit had been providing. She would learn quickly just how inept she was. But for now, when Dad praised her for all her help, she smiled and took the credit. Mistake. James 1:17 "Every good and perfect gift is from above, coming down from the father of heavenly lights." It is a tough pill to swallow at 13 to learn just how insignificant you are to the whole scheme of life. However, she was soon to learn that the pill once swallowed opened Lizbeth's eyes enabling her to go through the proverbial looking glass and slide down the rabbit hole.

Pricilla and Lizbeth had a 2-hour bus ride in the morning to school. Although school was only 30 min away, they were the first picked up, because they lived the farthest. They had assigned seats. Lizbeth sat across from this boy, Sean who was in Pricilla's class. Next to her was a girl named Sarah who slept the whole bus ride to school. Sean was the only entertainment on the bus. Since Lizbeth was a morning person, she was full of energy in the morning. Pricilla on the other hand was a night person. At night is when Pricilla thrived. So, on the long bus ride, Sean would tell jokes and talk to Lizbeth. Sean was a 10th grader and Lizbeth was in 7th. Lizbeth didn't think anything about Sean's attention. He was just an older boy, who was entertaining on the bus. At thirteen, Lizbeth had a huge crush on a boy in her class, Greg. Lizbeth could not bring herself to talk to him. Every time she tried to say Hi, something stupid came out. When he was around, she was a bumbling idiot. She would trip up steps, drop her books, walk into a pillar, you name it. If anyone could act stupid it was Lizbeth around Greg. She swore Greg never noticed her. But she noticed everything about him. He was popular while Lizbeth was not. He was outgoing while Lizbeth was quietly shy. He was funny while Lizbeth was serious.

He was everything that Lizbeth wasn't, and She was in love, although they never spoke.

Days on the bus were long, but Lizbeth looked forward to Sean's jokes, and he looked right into her eyes when he spoke. He noticed her. He would complement her on her outfit or her hairstyle, and he made Lizbeth feel noticed. But she never thought that he had any interest in her. He was so much older than her. Besides she had Greg, yes, the boy she never was able to talk to.

One morning, Lizbeth was sick and had to stay home from school. She tried with all her might to get up, the last thing she wanted was to stay home with her mom. But when her dad came in, not knowing she had concealed that she had thrown up twice in the middle of the night, and felt her head, he declared that she would have to stay home.

So, Lizbeth was banned from school that day and sentenced to a day in the state Lulu bin with her mother, Great! Dad reassured her that he didn't have to work real late and would try to come home early. Pricilla went off to the bus.

To this day, Lizbeth never really heard the full story of what happened on that bus, but when Pricilla got home from school, she was fit to be tied. Apparently, in Lizbeth's absence, Sean took the opportunity to ask Pricilla if she thought Lizbeth liked him. At first, Pricilla thought he was insinuating that Lizbeth was flirting with him and he didn't like it. But Sean had corrected her and asked

Pricilla if Lizbeth would want to date him. Hearing these words, Lizbeth thought yuck. He was like all mannish looking. She had no interest in him at all. She had Greg, the boy she could not even talk to. But Pricilla liked Sean. Who would have ever called that one? She never even talked to him……. OH…. Pricilla's Greg. Pricilla hated Lizbeth even more. *What a little bitch! Lizbeth thinks she is all that,* thought Pricilla.

Lizbeth tried to reassure Pricilla that she had no interest in Sean, but Pricilla's fury was a mini mom in size. Pricilla knew what to do. She would tell their mother. Mother would fix Lizbeth good. Pricilla proceeded to barge into the darkened room where the monster slept and woke the beast. She told her that Lizbeth was flirting with a boy on the bus who was 4 years older than her and acting like a slut. To enhance her story Pricilla exaggerated simple bus talk to flipping her hair, hiking up her skirt, and leaning forward to show her boobs. Lizbeth had to laugh at that one. At 83 pounds, Lizbeth did not even need a training bra. What boobs could she flash? Even if she had wanted to, Lizbeth was no Barbie, she was Skipper. Right there, Pricilla went too far, she made her story unbelievable. *Her mom should know this was all a lie*, she thought. The rantings of a jealous sister. Lizbeth didn't do anything, but just pass the time on the bus. Then Lizbeth said it, "What the F..k". She wasn't sorry for it. This was out of control. *I hate Pricilla*, she thought.

Lizbeth didn't realize how far her spiritual connection had fallen. Curse words, words of hate, against a sibling, it was Cain and Abel. Later when Lizbeth reflected on this time, she saw all of it clearly. It was Cain and Abel. Pricilla was jealous and had been rejected, not just by Sean, but by their dad as well. Pricilla wanted to take Lizbeth out. The Bible never said anything about Abel hating Cain. Just Cain hating Abel. Lizbeth took it to the next level. Pricilla was wrong but so was Lizbeth. Lizbeth now hated her sister, because of the jealousy Pricilla had for her. Well, that's a twist that only Satan could pull out of his hat. Lizbeth was being toyed with and she didn't even know it. But she would. God doesn't let us stay disconnected long. He will allow refinement to happen. First, it comes as a whisper, but if we don't listen, he will let the hits come. Lizbeth had slipped so far from Him now that she was surely going to get hit hard. And she was. Psalms 66:10 "For you God, have tested us. You have refined us, as silver is refined."

Pricilla had perfectly executed the monstrous side of their mom. Fury spewed out along with the metamorphosis of "The Eyes", but it was not toward Pricilla for being a jealous baby, but to Lizbeth, and full throttle.

"You whore! I knew you would turn out like a little whore." She grabbed Lizbeth by the hair and slapped her in the face. Lizbeth didn't know to protect her face or hold onto her head so her hair would not be ripped out. "You dirty little cunt. How dare you embarrass your family and act like a whore" She shoved Lizbeth to the ground and gave her several good kicks Lizbeth in the stomach. "Hope you never have children now", mom bellowed and left the room leaving Lizbeth hunched over on the floor coughing.

Lizbeth still was sick with a high fever, but none of that mattered. Dad was at work, so much for leaving early. Lizbeth could hear all kinds of banging upstairs and soon her mother emerged with a suitcase. Her mother grabbed the keys to the car in one hand suitcase in the other and stormed out the door. She entered again and grabbed a fist full of Lizbeth's hair and commanded her to get up. Did Lizbeth have a choice? Her mother had hair in tow, so Lizbeth had no choice but to follow. Her mother dragged her to the car and shoved Lizbeth's 83-pound body into the seat like she was a sack of potatoes. The final blow she looked right at her as she sat hovering in the car and spat in Lizbeth's face. "I never loved you, you dirty little whore. I will take you where you belong. And your dad, well he can find another piece of ass to F..k." What? Wait? How did this end up on her? Where was Mom taking her? To the Orphanage? She had always threatened she was going to get rid of her, was she carrying that threat out now? What would Daddy say? Would he even come to find her? And O my God what is she talking about, Dad? He can find another bleep bleep bleep...... Dad never touched me ever. What is Mom talking about? Is that what she thought Dad and her relationship was? Doing the nasty with her? Lizbeth wanted to throw up. But first, she had to have her wits about her. She needed to keep track of where she was. Pay attention, Lizbeth, she said to herself. Know where you are going.

Mom's diatribe in the car never stopped. Lizbeth did not even try to fight back, nor try to speak. She knew that the Being her mom was right now, could not be reasoned with. The ride took about an hour. Yes, Lizbeth was in Philadelphia. She recognized it because Dad on special occasions would get Chinese food from around here. She was near China Town she thought. Ok, ok, Lizbeth thought, this is it. This is the end. Dad would not even know where she was. Mom was certainly not going to tell him. Pricilla would be glad she was gone. So, this was it. Lizbeth scanned the area and saw the graffiti, the trash on the sidewalks, the run-down housing; yep she was going to be all alone on the streets in a very scary neighborhood.

Suddenly, her mom pulled over and commanded her to get out. Lizbeth tried to look into her mother's eyes to see if there was any semblance that her mom was in there. "Mom", she said. "Get the F..k out! You want to be a little whore; this is where the whores go. So you can F..k all the men you want. Now you can't F..k your father anymore and he can be my husband again." Mom screamed "MOMMY, I NEVER......" Lizbeth pleaded.

"Don't call me that! I am not and was never your mother." Mom said with no remorse in her voice.

"Mom, please. I love you. Don't do this. Dad has never touched me. That's gross Mom! What are you talking about? "Lizbeth retorted hoping some logic would settle in. "Get the f...k out of the car, or I will F..king kill you." Mom was serious. Lizbeth knew she had to comply.

To enhance your experience please pause at this time in reading and feel free to YouTube the following song.

Toby Mac, "Help is On the Way"

It may be midnight or midday
Never early, never late
He gon' stand by what He claim
Lived enough life to say
I heard your heart
I see your pain
Out in the dark
Out in the rain
Feel so alone
Feel so afraid
I heard you pray in Jesus' name
It may be midnight or midday
It's never early, never late
He gon' stand by what He claim
I've lived enough life to say
Help is on the way (roundin' the corner)
Help is on the way (comin' for ya)
Help is on the way (yeah, yeah)

I've lived enough life to say
Help is on the way
Sometimes it's days
Sometimes it's years
Some face a lifetime of falling tears
But He's in the darkness
He's in the cold
Just like the morning, He always shows
It may be midnight or midday
It's never early, never late
He gon' stand by what He claim
I've lived enough life to say
Help is on the way (roundin' the corner)
Help is on the way (comin' for ya)
Help is on the way (yeah, yeah)
I've lived enough life to say
Help is on the way
Well I've seen my share of troubles
But the Lord ain't failed me yet
So I'm holding on to the promise y'all
That He's rolling up His sleeves again
Said I've seen my share of troubles
But the Lord ain't failed me yet
We'll keep holding on to the promise y'all
That He's rolling up His sleeves again
Don't you know it
(Rolling up his sleeves again)
I can see him rolling
(Rolling up, rolling up)
Help is coming
(Rolling up his sleeves again)
It may be midnight or midday
He's never early, no never late
He gon' stand by what He claim
I've lived enough life to say
It may be midnight or midday

It's never early, never late
He gon' stand by what He claim
I've lived enough life to say
Help is on the way
Help is on the way (roundin' the corner)
Help is on the way

Lizbeth did not know what ignited all this anger in her mother. She really didn't even have time to think. She opened the door of the car and got out. Crying an uncontrollable sob, and shaking like a leaf, Lizbeth started to throw up on the side of the road. Her mother got out of the car. At first, Lizbeth thought, mom had come to her senses and was going to tell her to get back in, but no, Lizbeth's mother reached in the back seat for the suitcase and threw it at Lizbeth, just missing her head. As Lizbeth looked up, she saw her mother screech off and there she was, alone on the streets of Philadelphia. It was cold and Lizbeth was not wearing a coat. She was scared. She knew she was in a bad area of Philadelphia. She knew Dad was not even home from work. Was he still at work? Could she reach him there? She started crying hysterically. Shaking from the cold and the fear of all that had happened. Mom's car was nowhere in sight. Funny all those times Mom had gotten out of the car, Dad would follow her to make sure she didn't get hurt. Mom did not afford this same kind of concern for her.

Very quickly Lizbeth knew she could not stay where she was. She would be easy prey for anyone to grab her. She wiped her face and stood up. She decided to leave the suitcase behind, it made her look like an outsider and easy prey for any onlookers. Payphone, that's what I need, she thought, I must reach Dad before he leaves work. He worked in Manayunk, which was close. Payphone! I need a pay phone; she thought as she surveyed the area for one. There on the corner, only one block ahead was a pay phone. She walked with hastened speed, to call her daddy's work. Lizbeth had no money on her, so she had to make the call a collect call. The phone rang and rang, and just as she was about to hang up, she heard her dad's voice on the phone.

"Dad!", she yelled.

He could not hear her… the operator on the other end said. I have a collect call from …. Lizzie screamed "Lizzie". will you accept the charges?

Dad said yes, Lizzie broke down and cried. She cried so hard he could not even understand her. "Daddy help, please help me", she sobbed. After several attempts, Dad finally figured out that Lizzie was not at home and on the streets of Philadelphia.

He tried to calm Lizbeth down, she was hyperventilating now. He had to calm her down, so he screamed at her. Daddy never screamed at Lizzie. This snapped her to reboot her emotions.

"Lizzie, STOP, I won't be able to find you unless you calm down", dad barked!" She sniffled taking in deep shallow breaths, "OK! I am trying Daddy" Lizzie huffed trying to calm down. "Where are you?"

said her dad. "I don't know, kind of near where you get Chinese Food." Lizzie surmised.

"HOLY SHIT", her father said. "Ok, Ok, look for a street sign or something near you to describe to me so I can figure out where you are", dad questioned. His voice was tense and strained, Lizzie could tell he was stressed to the max. Daddy did care about her. He was trying to find her. Daddy did not want her gone. "OK Daddy I am looking", Lizzie was able to give him a street and a description of the things that were around her. "Now," said her dad. "I need you to look. Are there any stores or restaurants? Anyplace you can get off the street to be safe?" With that 4-letter word SAFE, reality smacked Lizzie in the face, yes she had to get someplace safe. *BE SAFE? RIGHT????* *I needed to be safe,* thought Lizzie. *STOP crying, you little baby. THINK Lizbeth. Think! OK* she spotted a diner, it was rough, but she would head there.

Dad said, "Ok that's my girl, you can do this. When we hang up, I want you to run to the diner. You look for a nice waitress and you just tell her that your Daddy is picking you up there. Don't tell her what happened Lizzie. Do you hear me? Don't tell her what happened. They will call the Police. WE DO NOT WANT THE POLICE INVOLVED. Did you understand babe? Wipe your face and pretend you are ok. DON'T CRY! BE STRONG! YOU CAN DO THIS!" I am leaving now; it is only 20 minutes from my work. OK?"

"Daddy I can't," she sobbed "I can't get my legs to move, and I peed my pants. I threw up and there is throw-up all over the bottom of my pants. I'm scared", she cried. "HONEY! CALM DOWN! you are my strong one. I know you can do this! YOU ARE MY STRONG ONE. I NEED YOU TO BE STRONG!" I will be there soon. I love you. …. Lizzie…" he said this time in a soft voice. "Yes, Daddy, I LOVE YOU TOO!" Lizzie sobbed back. That was it, those 3 little words. Her Dad loved her. Her dad was going to save her. Her dad was there. HE NEEDED HER TO BE THE STRONG ONE. She had to do this for him. "OK, Daddy! I will be good. I won't tell anyone what happened. I will be calm. I promise." Lizzie guaranteed. "Good girl. I knew you would. You are my good girl. Now go! Once you get to the diner you will be safe. Order something to eat. I will pay for it when I get there." Daddy hung up, but he was on his way. She would be ok. Lizzie wiped her tears and pulled back her hair, so it didn't look like she had been in a fight. Now what? She had peed her pants and thrown up on them. *THINK Lizbeth THINK* she thought. *THE SUITCASE.*

Lizbeth opened the door of the phone booth and ran to the suitcase. She opened it and there was a fresh pair of pants and underwear in it. She dodged behind a bush and changed her clothes leaving her soiled clothing behind. Then she ran to the diner. She ran like never before in her life. She stopped her sprint just before she opened the door. She did not want to go in like a bat out of hell.

She knew she could draw no extra attention to herself. *BE CALM,* she thought. *NO POLICE. TELL NO ONE. Make sure you act like this is normal. Come up with a story. THINK.... Ok got it.* Lizbeth pulled the door of the diner open as cool as cool could be. She looked presentable she thought. She hopped up onto a seat at the counter, smiled at the waitress, and asked for a menu. The waitress was looking around. Lizbeth suspected she was looking for an adult. So, Lizbeth beat her to the punch. "Hi, my dad is meeting me here can I order for him and myself, please?" Lizbeth looked the waitress square in the eyes. *BE BELIEVABLE* she said to herself. *Show no fear. Act like it is normal.*

The waitress was so nice. "Oh, Sure honey, of course you can." Lizbeth could tell that the waitress thought this was a little sketchy, so to seal the deal Lizbeth added. "Oh, my mom and dad don't get along (not a lie). She dropped me off (not a lie). Daddy is coming from work (not a lie)."

The waitress looked at Lizbeth with humor in her voice and said, "O girl, I know how that be! How about, I place your order now, and when your Daddy comes, I will put his order in." Lizbeth smiled; mission accomplished. She did not lie, and she kept her promise to Daddy. No one would know, and no police. Daddy would be happy with Lizbeth. She would do anything for him.

Sure enough, Daddy got there quickly. Lizbeth was not even upset anymore. The waitress was very funny and entertaining, and she looked Lizbeth in the eyes when they were talking. She complimented Lizbeth on her hair and told her she had the most beautiful eyes. She also told Lizbeth that she had never met such a well-behaved little girl. Lizbeth was in 7th grade but because of her size, she still looked like a little girl. The waitress made Lizbeth feel noticed.

Looking back. Lizbeth never called on GOD, but she knows He was there. She knew He was with her that day. She believed that the waitress was her guardian angel. The waitress was calm and commanding and so sweet to Lizbeth; She made Lizbeth feel safe. Lizbeth and her dad finished their meal, although Lizbeth did not eat much, as they left, the waitress turned to Lizbeth's dad and said, "You take care of her. She is a special one. She is going to do great things." Dad looked at the waitress not understanding, but as Lizbeth looked back on that night, she knows in her heart that the waitress was her guardian angel.

The ride home was quiet. Dad got a short version of what happened. She was exhausted. She was still feeling sick, and now all she wanted to do was sleep. Dad let her sleep. When they pulled into the driveway, Dad said wait here; he wanted to get the lay of the land on the home front before Lizzie came in. Mom's car was in the driveway. Lizbeth made a note to herself. Yep, Mom really left me there. She didn't care what happened to me. OK, hurtful, but it doesn't matter. Daddy loves me. A few short minutes went by, and

Dad returned, he had reported that Mom was asleep and to go straight upstairs.

Lizbeth, half sick, exhaustedly drug herself up the stairs and ran a short bath. She wouldn't be able to sleep with the pee and the throw-up still on her. The bath was warm, and it felt so good. She sunk her head under the water and lay there still while the warm water went around her head. She held her breath and blew a few bubbles. It was so peaceful. Then she held her breath a little longer and tried not to blow bubbles this time. It was calm, Hmmm, could she? She lifted her head and took a deep breath and then down she went to immerse herself in the warm water again. OK, this time don't blow bubbles, see how it feels. Warm water, calm, don't breathe. Is this what not being here would feel like? Could she just pass out under the water and that would, be it? She practiced again. This time was even better. She did not feel a sense of panic, she just felt the warmth of the water around her face. It felt good. Hold your breath. PEACE....

Lizbeth is not sure if she passed out or had fallen asleep, but all of a sudden, she heard HIM again. Yes, the one she had put on the shelf. He was showing up again. She heard HIS voice. "Lizbeth. STOP! Lift your head. This is not how your life ends. You are loved BY ME! You have a special job to do. You are mine. You don't get to choose when you die. I choose. NOW LIFT YOUR HEAD!" Swoosh, Lizbeth pulled her head out of the water, gasping for a breath of air. UGH, it had been so peaceful in that place. Why did she pick her head up?

When Lizbeth got out of the bathroom, everyone was asleep. She slipped into her dad's bathroom. Mom and Dad slept in separate rooms. There in the cabinet were pills Daddy took sometimes when he said his heart was racing. These pills helped Daddy's heart calm down, he had told her a few times when she saw him holding his wrist and taking his pulse. She grabbed the bottle and went into her bedroom. Remembering how she had felt in the tub, Peaceful, she poured a handful of the pills into her hand. God wouldn't deny her being at peace. This would be easier. She could take a few pills and then that would be it. Mom would be happy because she never wanted her. Pricilla would certainly be happy. Aww poor Daddy, he would miss her, but Mom was probably going to make her leave in the morning anyway. This way Daddy would not have to worry about her being on the streets. It was a win-win for everyone. Lizbeth looked at the pills in her hand, then thought of the voice in the bathtub, Him, the waitress, saying this is a special one, and her old Sunday school teacher's lesson. Then she prayed,
"The Lord is my shepherd..."

And God showed up. He told her again, that He loved her. This was not her time to join HIM. She had a job, and He knew she would complete this work. He told her he knew she would feel this way tonight, but it was necessary, she would be able to help others

73

someday. He told her she would be the first in her family for 6 generations to not have children that were abused. Her children would be the first of a new generation that would be raised to Love and Honor HIM. He was using her to break the chain of abuse. He would give her what she needed. TRUST ME, He said. And so, she did trust him that is. She put the pills away. She knew then just how far she had drifted from his peace. During these times she was going through turmoil, she never called on HIM. She vowed never again. I can't do it without HIM. That night she lay in her bed and said only 8 words. "I LOVE YOU LORD. I WILL TRUST YOU."

To enhance your experience please pause at this time in reading and feel free to YouTube the following song.

Francesca Battistelli *"He Knows My Name"*

He calls me chosen, free forgiven, wanted, child of the King

Spent today in a conversation
In the mirror face to face with
Somebody less than perfect
I wouldn't choose me first if
I was looking for a champion
In fact I'd understand if
You picked everyone before me
But that's just not my story
True to who You are
You saw my heart
And made
Something out of nothing

I don't need my name in lights
I'm famous in my Father's eyes
Make no mistake
He knows my name
I'm not living for applause
I'm already so adored
It's all His stage
He knows my name oh, oh
He knows my name oh, oh
I'm not meant to just stay quiet
I'm meant to be a lion
I'll roar beyond a song
With every moment that I've got
True to who You are
You saw my heart
And made
Something out of nothing
I don't need my name in lights
I'm famous in my Father's eyes
Make no mistake
He knows my name
I'm not living for applause
I'm already so adored
It's all His stage
He knows my name oh, oh
He knows my name oh, oh
His forever, held in treasure
I am loved
I don't need my name in lights
I'm famous in my Father's eyes
I don't need my name in lights
I'm famous in my Father's eyes
Make no mistake
He knows my name
I'm not living for applause
I'm already so adored

It's all His stage
He knows my name
He knows my name oh, oh
He knows my name

When Lizbeth woke up, her mom said nothing. There was no yelling, no telling her to leave, no memory that yesterday had ever happened...... to her. Surprisingly, Lizbeth was not angry. She was not mad at Pricilla for causing it. She wasn't mad at her mother for abandoning her on the streets of Philadelphia, she loved her dad even more because he saved her, and Jesus well, she was understanding him better as well. God was with us, but if we didn't try to have a relationship with Him, he would retreat. He did not force Himself on anyone. He was there and protected us, but He would let us have our way. She learned she did not like that feeling of not having Him so connected. So, she again walked outside and talked with Him. She sat at her window at night with the window open and talked to Him. She talked to Him before she went to bed, and she felt good.

Mommy was in a particularly good mood; she was readying for a wedding that was that weekend. It was the first Lizbeth had heard about it. When the invitation came her mother had RSVP'd no. Now apparently, they were all going. She laid an outfit out on Lizbeth's bed for her to wear, and one for Pricilla. She was like a little kid, excited and happy. Lizbeth couldn't remember seeing her mother like this. This was a family that Lizbeth had never heard about, but apparently, Mom wanted to make an impression. Mom popped her head into Lizbeth's room all cheery, "Practice a couple of songs, I want you and your sister to sing at the wedding" she said. What? Was Mom delusional? She wanted us to show up for this wedding and act like the Von Trapp family from Sound of Music. Any remnant of yesterday's antics was non-existent. It was like it never happened. Mom was expecting full conformity; hair, dress, and a performance; we all knew what the consequences would be for non-conformity. It actually was not hard to play along. This joyful mom full of excitement and energy was new. OK, we could play the Von Trapp family for an evening. Maybe this new version of Mom would stick around. Mom was acting like, well, a young girl; She was giddy and laughing and acting a bit shy with her family members at the wedding. She was quite charming. She was witty, fun, and happy… and she danced! At the table, she moved her head to the beat and rolled her shoulders; Lizbeth could see why Dad married her if this is how she was when they were dating. She was fun. Now was the time mom was waiting for; time to showcase her offspring. Her eyes were beaming as she boasted that Pricilla and Lizbeth had great voices. Everyone was intrigued and started chanting for the two girls to take the stage. They sang a medley of *Jeremiah Was a Bullfrog*, *The Night the Lights went out in Georgia*, and Together *Wherever we go*. Everyone cheered and hugged Mom giving her kudos for raising such charming girls. Mom was a hit, and she was beaming from ear to ear. She was different around this crowd, she talked in a sweet voice, and her laugh was infectious. Lizbeth had never seen her mom this happy. She wanted to burn the memory into her mind and never forget it. For that moment Lizbeth felt like they were a family.

Oh, what a night it was, Lizbeth did not want it to end. It was time to cut the cake, and everyone crowded around to see the festivities. An elderly Aunt came up to Lizbeth and gave her a piece of wedding cake. She said, "You take this home dear and put it under your pillow." "Under my pillow?" Lizbeth questioned. "Yes," said the elderly relative, "If you put a piece of cake under your pillow the night of the wedding you will dream about who you are going to marry." "WOW, I can't wait", said Lizbeth. She actually couldn't wait, she was not just being polite; she couldn't wait to go to sleep tonight to dream of Greg.

It was very late when they arrived home, Lizbeth ran up to her room, bursting with anticipation of dreaming about who she was going to marry. She placed the wrapped piece of cake under her pillow and was about to jump into bed to start her dream fest when she stopped. Hmm, the whole cake under her pillow seemed a little superstitious. She did not think God would like that. So, she decided to cover all bases and said a prayer. "Dear Lord, I trust you, in you, not in a piece of cake, so could you have me dream about whom I will marry? Thank you, Amen." she prayed. The next morning, she awoke with a big smile on her face, she had a wonderful dream. She saw him. She saw the guy she was going to marry; she saw her wedding dress. She was going to get married. But wait, who was it she thought. Was it him? Was it Greg? Ugh no it didn't really look like Greg; think Lizbeth think, was it anyone she knew? No, she could not place the face. All she remembered was that he looked like Speed Racer. No, he was not a cartoon, but he was a human version of what Speed Racer would look like. He was of thin build, light eyes, and black hair. At first, Lizbeth was upset that she didn't know anyone that fit the bill but then resolved to just be happy that she was indeed going to marry. She could not wait. She was going to make sure she was a good wife and mother. "Thank you, God, for your promise", she said. She remembered what he had told her the night before when she had contemplated ending her time here. She would marry, and her kids would not be abused. Knowing this gave her happiness. She couldn't wait to grow up. ***Proverbs 37:4*** *"Delight yourself in the Lord, and He will give you the desire of your heart."*

Lost or Found

By this time Lizbeth was 14 and found herself depending more and more on God. She prayed often and she found that the more she looked to Him the better things went for her in her life. Around her neck hung a small little gold cross that she received from her grandmother when she was christened as a baby. She wore it from the time she was little and never took it off. Lizbeth was very active at school. She played field hockey in the fall, swam in the winter, and did gymnastics or track in the spring. Playing sports gave Lizbeth an outlet to be outside, away from her mom, and keep in shape. Anorexia was always right around the corner for her. She had to work at keeping it at bay. Somedays she forced herself to eat something fattening to prove a point that it was gone.

She was pretty athletic and although was never the star of a team, she held her own. Her mom and dad never came to any of her sporting competitions, or games. Lizbeth would see the other student's parents on the sidelines, and the pain of it caused tears to arrive as no one was there for her. She would grab the cross around her neck rub it and she felt strong. This ritual she believed helped her run faster, play harder, and feel confident. Good thing, right? Was it the object of the cross that gave her this newfound power, or was it God who gave her it?

As Lizbeth prayed and clung to the cross that was around her neck, she found she was rubbing it and counting on its protection, and the success that IT brought her. OOOh, noo bad thing. This went on for about a solid month. Every time Lizbeth felt stressed, she rubbed the cross. If Lizbeth wanted a good grade on a test, she rubbed the cross. If Lizbeth wanted to play well during a game, she rubbed the cross. If Lizbeth was on her way home, she rubbed the cross. On and on the ritual continued, until one night as Lizbeth sat at her window and was pouring her heart out to God, she looked at the sky and heard Him again. "TAKE IT OFF". At first, she was confused, but she recognized the voice, the feeling, and the conviction given, it was truly Him. He was not asking her to take off the cross but COMMANDING her to take it off. Could she be wrong? All these times she thought HE had spoken to her, was it, not Him? Why? Would God want her to take off such a magical ...... OOOH? Yes, the Lord had opened Lizbeth's eyes that she was using the innocent little cross that represented what HE had done for her, as a good luck charm, a talisman. It was so innocent. It happened so fast and so innocuously, that the little cross became a stumbling block for Lizbeth. It wasn't the cross that gave her anything. He gave her the talents. He gave her success. He gave her protection, not a little gold cross around her neck. Lizbeth removed the cross and placed it in her draw. To this day, she never placed a cross around her neck again. She feared that she might always fall prey to the power of using it as a talisman. *Proverbs 16:3 "Commit your work to the Lord, and your plans will be established."*

Several days passed, and Lizbeth felt stronger. She felt free. She was not tied to rubbing that little cross. She had heard Him again. He was with her. He was listening. He was there and making sure she was doing right by Him. All she had to do was listen. She would always listen to His voice. She would do anything for Him if He asked her to. "I love you Lord", she said inside her head and heart, and she walked outside and looked at the sky. He was there. He was out there, in her, everywhere. God was literally everywhere, and she could see His hand in everything now.

Unspoken, "Reason"

This year's felt like four seasons of winter
And you'd give anything to feel the sun
Always reaching, always climbing
Always second guessing the timing
But God has a plan, a purpose in this
You are His child and don't you forget
He put that hunger in your heart
He put that fire in your soul
His love is the reason
To keep on believing
When you feel like giving up
When you feel like giving in
His love is the reason
To keep on believing

If we could pull back the curtain of Heaven
We would see His hand on everything
Every hour, every minute, every second, He's always been in it
Don't let a shadow of a doubt take hold (take hold)
Hold on to what you already know
He put that hunger in your heart (hunger in your heart)
He put that fire in your soul (fire in your soul)
His love is the reason
To keep on believing
When you feel like giving up (feel like giving up)
When you feel like giving in (giving in)
His love is the reason
To keep on believing (yeah)
(His love is) it's the reason
(His love is) it's the reason
His love is the reason (ooh)
He's the peace in the madness
That you can't explain
He's the hope in the heartbreak
The rest in the suffering
He's closer than the air you breathe
From the start to the end to the in between
Don't you dare doubt even for a minute
What He started in you
Yeah, He's gonna finish
He put that hunger in your heart (hunger in your heart)
He put that fire in your soul (fire in your soul)
His love is the reason (Your love, Your love)
To keep on believing (just keep on believing)
When you feel like giving up (feel like giving up)
When you feel like giving in (oh) (giving in)
His love is the reason (Your love, Your love)
To keep on believing (yeah)

(His love is)
It's the reason (His love is)
(His love is)
It's the reason (His love is)
His love is the reason (His love is)
It's the reason (His love is)
It's the reason
His love is the reason, hey, hey

Just as she walked inside the house, feeling so empowered by Him. Feeling so connected to Him she glided into the kitchen where her mom lay in wait. She saw the smile on Lizbeth's face, it set off a trigger in her mother. Her mother scrutinized her like she was trying to figure out why her daughter looked joyful. Then her eyes zoned onto Lizbeth's neck. It was like an Eagle spotting prey from a great distance. Her mother saw the cross-less, bare neck of Lizbeth, and THE EYES changed. "I Knew it! She spat. I knew you were a bad seed. Was it burning your skin?" her mother hissed. Lizbeth knew immediately where her mother was going with this. Her mom was assuming that because Lizbeth was not wearing her cross; Lizbeth was declaring she was not a Christian anymore. It was soooooo far from the truth. O how she wanted to tell her what HE had told her. She wanted to tell her mom just what God meant to her. But she couldn't bring herself to say a word. Lizbeth had become silent again. She stared at her mother like a deer in headlights. Her feet Frozen to the floor, Lizbeth just looked at her.

That was a fatal posture for Lizbeth to assume when THE EYES were present. Her mother took the stance as an act of defiance, an act of aggression, a stance that needed to be submitted, and her mother was the one to do it. Lizbeth did not know why she was looking straight into her mother's eyes, she knew better. She was thinking about the real reason she had taken off the cross and what a blessing it was. It was not Lizbeth going backward in her faith, she was moving forward. She was processing the possibility of defending herself. She was contemplating if it would make a difference if it would calm the beast. She couldn't believe this was happening! She didn't even realize she had done it. Lizbeth blew it, she made eye contact with THE EYES.

Mom screamed to Lizbeth's dad, "GET DOWN HERE NOW! Pricilla! GET DOWN HERE", screamed her mother. You could hear them coming down the steps assuming their positions in front of Mom. *What now?* Thought Dad. *Usually, it was Pricilla that was causing the commotion, this time it was Lizzie?* Lizbeth's mother grabbed her by the arm, digging her nails into the back of her arm. She presented her to her dad and sister. "Look!" her mother directed as she ripped Lizbeth's hair away from her chest. At first, Dad saw nothing. Frustrated her mother grabbed Lizbeth around the back of her neck and shoved her closer to her dad. "See her neck? WHAT IS MISSING? YOU ASSHOLE?" Dad was still clueless. "THE F..King CROSS is gone," mom screeched with frustration. "I told you this one was a bad seed. I told you to be careful of the quiet one. I told you she would be a child of the world. I was right! Should have left her in Philadelphia." Mom dictated. There it was again. It rolled out of mom's mouth like it was nothing. *Mom remembered that she had left her there, so noted* Lizbeth thought. Lizbeth could feel her face grow hot. Her pulse was throbbing in her head. She was not even hurt at this point. She was angry. She was about to scream. She was about to say the tabu words "You are nuts. You are a nut job." She rubbed her thumbnail with her forefinger, she often did this to try to calm down. She looked at her dad. She was looking for help. She was looking for him to say something. Anything. Just step-up Dad and save me………. Nothing. ……. He did nothing…… SHOCKING……He wouldn't even look at her. Pricilla had a smile on her face. She was enjoying this. Someone else was getting Mom's wrath. She was waiting for Lizbeth to fight back…… nothing…… then Pricilla tried to bait her… "See Mom, I told you, Lizbeth is really a bad girl. She isn't quiet and innocent, she took the cross off cause she doesn't want God." Her sister stood there with her arms folded in front of her waiting for the fireworks to follow. Pricilla was not left wanting.

For the last 6 months, Mom had been occupying her time watching The Jim Bakker Show. It was a "religious" talk show… totally fake, but Mom was addicted to it. That is all she watched and now simple shows like the Brady Bunch were banned from their home. Lizbeth's house was becoming "sickly religious". There is a difference between religion and faith. This show was later taken off the air, and Jim Bakker and his wife were indicted for eight counts of mail fraud, 15 counts of wire fraud, and one count of conspiracy. It was estimated that they had stolen 158 million dollars from their followers. Anyway, fake show, fake religion, but Mom was hooked on it.

Pricilla continued, yah de dah de dah is all Lizbeth heard. Lizbeth looked at her sister with a look saying "WHAT THE HELL?" *OK, Pricilla I see what you are*, Lizbeth thought. *I knew I could never trust you. You have never been a sister to me,* Lizbeth's thoughts continued. Lizbeth looked out the window and saw the sky... She knew who she needed and who to call on and she did. She talked to Him. "Lord, you know why I took off the cross. You know it was not for the reason they think. What do I say? What do I do?" The answer came…... "DO NOTHING" Exodus 14:14 " The Lord will fight for you, and you have only to be silent."

A sudden feeling of peace came over her. She did not hear any additional words from God, but she knew what He was asking. The battle was not to be fought now. He knew she had taken the cross off because she was listening to Him. That is all that matter. So, Lizbeth did it; she remained silent. Her mother rattled on and on with all kinds of "lovely" adjectives about Lizbeth. Lizbeth just turned her attention to the sky and all she could hear was the likening of the teacher's voice in the Charlie Brown specials. "Wah wah wah.... Wah wah wah...." Her mother then got out the Wesson oil from under the counter, she poured some on her hands and rubbed them together. Her mother placed her oil-dripping hands-on Lizbeth's face and harshly rubbed the oil all over her head and hair. "Satan GET OUT!" her mother commanded. It was just how her mother had seen it done on that fake tv show she was always watching.

Is she kidding? Lizbeth thought she thinks she might have even rolled her eyes. No one saw, thank GOD. Ugh! now she had to wash her hair. *That was so far from a spiritual experience,* Lizbeth thought. In fact, Lizbeth thought, *if God hadn't given me such a special showing of HIS Presence all these years, she might have turned to team Satan at that moment.* But, no God was hers and she was His, and she would follow His command, "Say Nothing". So, she didn't say a word. The peace that came to Lizbeth far exceeded the experience. The sun shone through the kitchen window and Lizbeth could feel the warmth on her face. It felt good. The timing was perfect, her mother saw the sun shining on Lizbeth's face and the peace radiating from Lizbeth and thought her whole demon Exorcist was successful. Mission accomplished her mother thought she had taken the devil out of her daughter. "Praise the Lord", her mother yelled, as she skipped around the kitchen and into the dining room. *OMG,* Lizbeth thought this is like a scene from "Carrie".

There are times when we are meant to fight and times when it is better to be silent. Only fight a battle if you think your words will make a difference. If your words are going to fall on hardened hearts, or hearts that will twist the truth, Let go and Let God. That is what Lizbeth learned from this experience. God had protected her heart and soul from being tainted by such an ungodly display of religion. To this day she never told her family why she had taken off that cross, and she has never put a cross around her neck again.

To enhance your experience please pause at this time in reading and feel free to youtube the following song.

Casting Crowns, "Who am I"

Who am I, that the Lord of all the earth
Would care to know my name, would care to feel my hurt?
Who am I, that the Bright and Morning Star
Would choose to light the way for my ever wandering heart?
Not because of who I am, but because of what You've done
Not because of what I've done, but because of who You are
I am a flower quickly fading, here today and gone tomorrow
A wave tossed in the ocean (ocean), a vapor in the wind
Still, You hear me when I'm calling, Lord, You catch me when I'm falling
And You've told me who I am
I am Yours, I am Yours
Who am I, that the eyes that see my sin
Would look on me with love and watch me rise again?
Who am I, that the voice that calmed the sea
Would call out through the rain and calm the storm in me?
Not because of who I am, but because of what You've done

Not because of what I've done, but because of who You are
I am a flower quickly fading, here today and gone tomorrow
A wave tossed in the ocean (ocean), a vapor in the wind
Still, You hear me when I'm calling, Lord, You catch me when I'm
falling
And You've told me who I am (I am)
I am Yours
Not because of who I am, but because of what You've done
Not because of what I've done, but because of who You are
I am a flower quickly fading, here today and gone tomorrow
A wave tossed in the ocean (ocean), a vapor in the wind
Still, You hear me when I'm calling, Lord, You catch me when I'm
falling
You've told me who I am (I am)
I am Yours
I am Yours, I am Yours, oh
Whom shall I fear? Whom shall I fear?
'Cause I am Yours, I am Yours

Puppy Love Sixteen

As the year proceeded, life returned to its normal state of affairs. Mom's episodes were still consistent. Lizbeth spent most of her time by herself in her room or doing things with her dad. Things at school were good. Lizbeth was good at History and found herself in an upperclassman History class. She was the only 10th grader in the class, and she sat next to a boy named Jake. Jake was an eleventh grader, but he knew Pricilla, Lizbeth's sister. He told her he was in two of Pricilla's classes the previous year. Jake was funny and pretty cute, but more importantly, he was very attentive to Lizbeth, and would often walk her to her next class. One day Pricilla came home from school and told Lizbeth that Jake liked her. Pricilla was being nice. Lizbeth was guarded. *Had hell frozen over*, she thought. Why was Pricilla being nice? Pricilla said, "He is actually, a really nice guy. Do you like him? Lizbeth was afraid to answer the question. The last time a boy was involved she was carted off to Philadelphia to live among the homeless. Was this a trap? Pricilla then said, "Well if you like him, I will help you be able to go out with him. I can start telling Mom and Dad about him and how great this boy is, and then later we can say he liked you and wants to ask you out. Let me know, ok?" Lizbeth felt like she was in the Twilight Zone. Was she in an alternate universe? Pricilla was being helpful and nice. What was in it for her? Why was she so willing to help?

The thing was, Lizbeth wasn't sure if she liked Jake. What about Greg? She still had a major crush on Greg, but nothing had changed on that front. He still didn't know she existed, and her bumbling idiot routine with him continued. Jake on the other hand liked her. He gave her lots of attention. Lizbeth decided "*A bird in the hand,*" so she started to think about Jake to see if she could like him.

He was easy to like actually. He stared at her like she was the only person in the room. When he walked her to classes his hand would occasionally graze her hand. He would joke with her and bring her little goodies to class. One day it would be gum, the next day licorice, Lizbeth's favorite candy, how did he know? Another day it was a new hair ribbon. Lizbeth had to admit, the attention was starting to wear her down. Jake was stepping up to the plate, unlike Greg who never really looked in her direction. Lizbeth was also very comfortable talking to Jake. She did not feel like a bumbling idiot. They had real conversations and was able to be herself with him. She felt comfortable with him. Is being comfortable a different kind of like? Lizbeth was looking for love, not like.

Lizbeth continued her friendship with Jake, he was playing the game perfectly. He was patient. It was like he knew that Lizbeth wasn't ready yet, and he was willing to wait. He didn't ask her out, he had a way of presenting innuendos of liking her, but never saying too much to scare Lizbeth off. So, by the time Valentine's Day rolled around, Lizbeth was definitely beginning to consider Jake more than a friend. He asked for her phone number, and he would call her late at night to talk. Lizzie enjoyed their late-night convos, and it was during one of these light night talks, Jake started to call Lizbeth, Lizzie. This took Lizzie's comfort zone to a whole other level. Daddy called her Lizzie, and she liked being called that; this gave Jake an edge calling her Lizzie made her feel warm. Jake had all the right moves.

For Valentine's Day, the school sold flowers to send to classmates. You could send a red carnation for love, pink for friendship, and white for innocence. There was also a card you could include with a written note. Lizbeth dreaded Valentine's Day. It always made her feel empty in a way. Her two friends and she would always send each other a flower, pink of course. They did this ritual every year, so they did not have to sit in classes while every other girl got a flower. Lizbeth walked into History class with 2 pink flowers. Jake was intrigued and a little jealous. *Who was sending her flowers?* He thought. Then it happened. In came the Valentine messenger. "Lizzie?" they called. Lizbeth raised her hand; she was red in the face and was holding back a smile. The deliverer gave her 2 flowers. One white, and one red with only one note. The two flowers were from the same person. Your secret admirer, it read, "One red and one white, "Cause I honestly love you." It was the title of Lizbeth's favorite song by Olivia Newton-John. How clever. By the wit of it, and it was addressed to "Lizzie", Lizbeth suspected it

had to be from Jake. But, after the delivery, he teased her
relentlessly to find out who sent her the flowers. He also tried to see
the card. Did that mean it was not from him? If it was from him, he
was being very coy about it. Besides whom else calls her Lizzie?
Could it be from Greg? she thought. Did she want it to be from Greg
or Jake? As she sat in class, she tried to analyze the answer to that
question.Who did she want the Valentine to be from? Greg would
not call her Lizzie. It had to be from Jake she resolved. Yes, she was
happy with that choice and decided that it was Jake, she wanted it to
be from.

As Jake walked her to her next class, she flirted with him,
she smiled and looked at him from a side glance and flipped her hair
a little. When their hands grazed as they walked, this time she let her
hand linger. He looked at her and noticed a difference. Then she
looked at him and said, "I thought maybe…. She paused…. you had
sent the flowers?" He turned and leaned close to her, slowly backing
her into the locker. He put his arm up and leaned against the locker.
Lizbeth thought he might try to kiss her, so she looked away but
then looked back. He said, "Why? would you like the flowers to be
from me?" She was uncomfortable, she didn't want to answer. He
put his hand to her face and made her look at him. Lizzie, did you
want me to send you a flower today?" The fact is, she did. She did
want him to send her a flower, but it said it was from a secret
admirer and she did not want to commit to wanting one from him if

he hadn't sent it. So, she did all she could and mustered up a response, "Tell me first if you sent it," he laughed and backed away, she laughed back and walked into her class. Hmm. He didn't say he did, but he didn't say he didn't either.

Things at home were going ok. Mom had gotten her first job ever. She was working in a women's boutique. She really enjoyed it. Her monstrous moods had diminished, she was decently pleasant, and things were going better. That night, right on time, Jake called Lizzie. She decided to jump to the chase, and asked, "How did you know that was my favorite song?" She thought that would be a clever way of catching Jake off guard. It did and he replied, "You told me one night on the phone" "Ah ha", Lizzie laughed, "I gotcha. You did send the flowers. Why didn't you tell me?", Lizbeth questioned. He said quietly, "When I asked you if you wanted me to send you one? Why didn't you answer." She got it. He was afraid she might not like him. He had been trying to find out if she did.

Lizbeth had her first date with Jake on her 16th birthday. Her sister did go to bat for her and told her parents that he was a very respectful guy. She even added, if he was older, she would date him. Hm.... Lizbeth still did not understand why Pricilla was being so helpful, but gift horse and mouth kind of thing, who was she to question? With Mom's better moods, and having a job, this was good timing.

Before Jake came to pick her up that night, he called to see what color she was wearing. Lizzie crinkled her nose at the thought. He was not going to try to match her, was he? She thought that was a little too cutesy. Whatever, she was going on her first date. Jake showed up, with three flowers, one lavender to match Lizzie's outfit, and 2 white roses, one for Lizzie's mom and one for Pricilla. "What a charmer!" Mom and Pricilla were simply giddy. Hook line and sinker for them, Dad on the other hand was not sold. When Jake entered the house and handed Lizzie the flower, he called her "Lizzie." Dad did not like this familiarity, *this kid is he forward, calling Lizbeth, Lizzie,* Dad thought. Dad shook Jake's hand hard and leaned into Jake's personal space as if to intimidate him. It worked, when Lizzie and Jake got in the car he said, "Your dad doesn't like me." Lizbeth reassured him that was not the case, but she inwardly wondered what was up with Dad. Lizbeth was allowed out for 3 hours. She had to be home by 9:00, so that ruled out a movie. Jake took her to a chip and putt, and ice cream after. They were home on the dot at 9:00, and he was allowed to stay till 9:30. At 9:25 Lizbeth's Dad yelled into the room that it was time for Jake to get ready to leave. OK…

Lizbeth walked Jake to the door. She was nervous that he might kiss her. She had never kissed anyone and wasn't sure if she wanted to kiss him yet. As they headed to the back door. Jake turned around took her hand and planted her with a very not first kiss kind of kiss. As he headed out the door, she thought yuck. Is that kissing? Maybe she didn't like him like that? She thought about the movies and wanted that sweet, give-you-goosebumps type kiss that makes your foot pop up in the back leaving you mesmerized and all dreamy. Then an even more scary thought entered her head. What if she was a bad kisser? Maybe he was thinking, wow, he didn't like her the way he thought he did. The one thing Lizbeth was certain of was she did not want to lose the attention Jake gave her. She knew that wasn't fair. She wanted him to like her, but she wasn't as sure how much she liked him. She also thought of the dream she had that night after the wedding. Jake definitely did not fit the bill. If anything, he was the antithesis of the guy in her dream that she was destined to marry.

Later that night Jake called her. A sense of relief ran through her, ok she wasn't so horrible of a kisser that he never called her again, and he still liked her. She wanted to tell him how she felt about the kiss, she just didn't know how to. Her years of silence, and quiet conformity, made her submissive, she didn't like that. She thought *I have to work on my voice, I have to learn to stand up for myself.* The end of the school year was approaching, and Jake had his junior prom. Lizbeth was not allowed to go with him. Her dad was the one who said no. What is up with Dad and Jake she thought? Dad confessed to nothing when she asked him if he didn't like Jake. He said she was a 10th grader and Jake was in 11th grade.

He was not going to have his daughter go to a prom at 16. Even though several of the girls in her class were invited to go, Lizbeth was disappointed but did not push it. Jake went to the prom by himself, he just hung out with friends and had a good time. The prom was over at 11:00, Jake promptly called her at 11:20. Lizzie, thought *good sign.*

Summer was in full swing; Jake was asking her out every Friday and Saturday night. The two started to assume they would be doing something those nights and often would talk about things they were going to do months in advance. The kissing got better, and Lizbeth definitely decided she liked Jake. Dad on the other hand did not. He had become downright rude when Jake would come and pick her up. Mom was acting ok, but Lizbeth did not spend too much time at the house, she didn't want to push it. Pricilla maintained her support of Jake and Lizbeth till the day of reckoning arrived. Pricilla had pledged her allegiance to help and now she wanted to get compensated for her success.

Lizbeth was readying herself for her date, when Pricilla entered her room, without so much as a knock on the door, she eyed Lizbeth up and down and said, "I will be going with you guys on your date tonight. Actually, I will be going out with both of you anytime I feel like it." "WHAT?", Lizbeth's eyes said it all. "HELL NO!". "That's right!" Pricilla continued, "If I feel like going out, I WILL BE GOING!" she crossed her arms in front of her to prove that the decision was final, and her face was smug, and her EYES had a vague familiarity to them. Lizbeth was not going to be controlled or manipulated by her. It was one thing to submit to their mother, but quite another to submit to Pricilla. Lizbeth did not care about the cost.

Lizbeth looked at her sister and said, "If you are going, there will be no date, I will call it off." Pricilla's eyes squinted up as she sized up Lizbeth's face to see if she was calling her bluff. Pricilla saw a different Lizbeth, not the silent sister she had known. Pricilla saw the fight, resolve, and determination in her sister, which only made Pricilla ready for a fight, and she knew just how to win. She had beaten Lizbeth in the past, she would get her goat again. Out the door she spun, as she left, she yelled into Lizbeth, "Just wait and see what happens…." Followed by a sick laugh. It was almost Deja vu for Lizbeth, why was that so familiar…. Yes. Pricilla acted like her mother. Either Pricilla had learned from the best, or Pricilla was continuing her transformation into a mini mom and Lizbeth had an intimation which one it was. Lizbeth quieted herself to try to ascertain what plan Pricilla was executing. Lizbeth stood in her room and could hear Pricilla approach the beast downstairs. "Loud Sigh… pause Loud Sigh!" Pricilla was setting the stage. She sat on the chair near their brooding mother. LOUD SIGH again. Pricilla drew her knees to her chest and started to bite her fingernails. She knew nail biting would be noticed by the beast. "STOP, biting your nails", Mom barked. There were certain triggers that would always get Mom's furnace blaring, nail biting was one of them. Pricilla Sighed Loudly again. "What's your problem?" Mom rebuked. That was Pricilla's cue, "Well, I wasn't going to say anything, but I am just worried about Lizbeth. I mean Jake is a whole year older than her. He is a nice guy, but he is a guy. I am just worried Lizbeth might not be able to handle him." The monster was listening and intrigued. Pricilla had played both Lizbeth and the monster into her hands. Pricilla continued hesitantly like she did not want to suggest what she was about to suggest, then she went for the kill. "Maybe, it would be a good idea, if I started going on dates with them. It would keep Lizbeth safe." Mom liked it. Lizbeth was a little whore after all. This was a good idea. Pricilla sealed the deal by adding a little sniffle and wiped her eyes in earnest to show genuine concern for her sister. As if Pricilla could sense her victim was near, she turned around to see Lizbeth standing in the doorway. Pricilla slowly puckered her lips and mouthed the final blow to her sister. "I told you so!" Pricilla had won.

Lizbeth was boiling mad; she could feel the heat in her face and her hands balled into fists. She was going to explode. Then she looked up and saw the cat-like sneer on her sister's face. She would not give Pricilla satisfaction. As Lizbeth entered the room her mother gave the instructions that Pricilla will be joining them on their dates. Lizbeth knew better than to fight back. She looked at her mom and said, "Oh sure Mom that is a great idea, I was going to suggest that a couple of times, I just... pause... I never suggested it 'cause I didn't want Pricilla to hang out with people so much younger than her. I know how you don't like when she acts too young..." She had done it; Lizbeth had flipped the table in her favor. Mom was always calling Pricilla immature. Lizbeth was ruthless at this point. She thought, *what is good for the goose is good for the gander.* "I did not want her to be embarrassed or feel that she didn't have a... date," Lizbeth continued to seal the deal. Yes, Lizbeth put the nail in the coffin, Pricilla's coffin. Now Pricilla's smug face went wicked, she seethed at Lizbeth. Lizbeth never laid eyes on her sister. She knew better than to arouse Pricilla's temper further. She did not offer her a knowing glance as Pricilla had given her. Lizbeth was only trying to maintain the sanctity of her relationship with Jake. She was not trying to prove that she could beat her sister at her own game. There was part of Lizbeth that liked she could be ruthless however, it meant that she was not this little submissive girl that people could walk all over, but there was another part of her that saw the warning sign. There was even a part of her that felt bad for Pricilla. And here it came, the results of Lizbeth's cunning, she counted to herself 10, 9, 8, 7, 6... Pricilla crucified herself without Lizbeth anyway. Did Lizbeth have to set her up for the fall that bad? Mother had processed Lizbeth's words and bought the argument which launched the campaign against Pricilla. Mom was up with guns loaded. *"You Baby!"* Mom directed her anger to Pricilla. *"You just did that because you couldn't get a date on your own. You want to hang out with your dumb baby sister…"* That was it! Pricilla and Mom were doing their thing, Lizbeth backed out of the room and readied herself for her date. Crisis averted, for now. At least now she understood why Priscilla had been so helpful to get her and Jake together. Pricilla wanted to be included in the dates, but why? Why would someone want to be the third wheel? Then she remembered, "In fact, if he were older, I would date him." Pricilla had said as one of her tactical maneuvers…. Pricilla liked Jake. Lizbeth remembered where Pricilla's jealousy had led her before to the streets of Philadelphia, she would have to tread lightly on Pricilla's feelings. Lizbeth took the win and basked in the relief that Pricilla was not going on her date with Jake. When Jake and Lizbeth stopped for ice cream that night, she bought some for Pricilla as a peace offering. Greedily Pricilla took the prize. A peace treaty had been established. Pricilla often got treats after Lizbeth's dates with Jake. Pricilla kept the peace.

      Pricilla's stratagem did have consequences. The next day after school, Lizbeth's mom was there to pick her up. At first, Lizbeth was surprised and thought something had happened, but her mother simply said, "You have a doctor's appointment." This was strange because Dad usually made all the arrangements and took both Lizbeth and Pricilla to the doctor, but Mom was doing better these days, maybe Dad was handing off some of the duties to her. As they pulled into the parking lot, Lizbeth saw it was an OBGYN doctor. Her mom said that since Lizbeth was 16 and hadn't got her period but once, she needed the doctor to make sure all was ok. All sounded on the up and up. When they called her name, her mother got up with her and went into the examination room. Lizbeth did not know at this time what kind of exam it was going to be. The nurse came in and gave Lizbeth a robe and invited her mother to wait in the waiting room. The nurse assured her mom that she would be called in once the doctor was finished. That apparently was not in her mother's plan. Her mother abruptly said, "NO, I will not be leaving, I will stay for the exam." The nurse looked at Lizbeth as if to ask, "Is that ok?" Lizbeth shook her head. The nurse looked at Lizbeth, and said, "If there is anything you want to discuss with the doctor privately let me know." Lizbeth nodded again. Mom looked at Lizbeth and then the nurse suspiciously, "There will be no private conversations with the doctor," mom retorted. The nurse rolled her eyes and closed the door behind her. Lizbeth was still clueless at this point about what kind of exam was going to be performed. Not that it would have mattered, but had she known she would not have nodded for her mom to be present. It would have been a battle Lizbeth would not have won anyway.

The doctor was a very pleasant woman, she swooshed in with a file with Lizbeth's name on it. She asked a bunch of questions. When was her last period? Lizbeth told her she had 1 period and got sick. That was over 6 months ago. The doctor explained to Lizbeth and her mom that because Lizbeth's body fat was so low, it often affects their period. She said that they would watch it and she did want to give Lizbeth an exam and make sure everything seemed to be in working order. Now, Lizbeth found out what kind of exam she would be getting. CRAP! Mortifying to the max.

At this point, the doctor asked Lizbeth's mother to leave, which was promptly refused. Again, the doctor looked at Lizbeth for the go-ahead, and Lizbeth just nodded. She was humiliated, and the doctor sensing her discomfort told her mother to move and position herself at Lizbeth's head. *OK, not a fun experience,* Lizbeth thought, *how often do girls have to get this done*? She was trying not to think about it when her mother boldly asked the doctor a question. "Is my daughter still a virgin?" The doctor looked shocked and almost jumped back. She declined to answer the question at first but then was thwarted by her mom's overly spirited assertion. "I am her mother, she is a minor, and I have the right to all information. Now! I am asking you if my daughter is still a Virgin?" Humiliation to mortified at lightning speed, though Lizbeth. She lay, legs in stirrups, exposed for the world to see, and now her mother was fighting with the doctor as to whether Lizbeth was a whore or not? Lizbeth interrupted their verbal altercation and told the doctor it was ok for her to divulge the information to her mother. The doctor disgustedly looked at Lizbeth's mother with a look of disdain and reported, "Yes, your daughter is still a virgin." Her mother looked pleased. Then her forehead crinkled into a frown, her eyes narrowed, and she rebuked Lizbeth saying, "Don't think you are off the hook. I will bring you in here every year and ask the same question. The day the answer is no, I will cart you off to the street in Philadelphia. YOU KNOW I WILL DO IT!" WAIT! WHAT! did she say? Mom did remember taking her to Philadelphia. She did remember leaving me on those streets that night. Game changer, not only could Mom control herself, but she also remembered the things she did. Mom offered no apologies, she wasn't sorry. Lizbeth tucked this new intel deep in her heart. She did not know when she would want to revisit it.

Having gotten the job done, Lizbeth's mom left the room satisfied with the outcome. She had confirmed that Lizbeth was not yet the whore she thought she would become, and a message was sent to her daughter, "Legs shut, or you are out!" The doctor's eyes welled with tears, as she looked at Lizbeth, "I am so sorry honey. You know you can come in here anytime or call with any questions and I do not have to tell your mother." It's fine Lizbeth said, but it wasn't fine, she was mortified on one hand and furious at the new knowledge she had gained of her mother. Lizbeth's experience at the doctor, ensured no guy would be touching her. She knew her mom meant business. For Lizbeth, this was not just a scare tactic that some parents would do. For Lizbeth, it was a real, and vital threat. The Chastity Belt had been secured.

Jake and Lizbeth continued dating and now it had been 9 months since their first date. Eventually, when some of their kissing had gotten a little too heated, Lizbeth told Jake about the events at the doctor's office, what her mom had said, and that "IT" was a hard NO. With her heart pounding in her chest, she had given him an out. If he wanted to break up with her, she would understand. She felt she was going to throw up as she waited for his reply. Would he break up with her over this? Lots of couples were doing it, and they were not dating as long as they were. How patient could he be? To her relief, Jake was patient. He said he loved her, not just to have "THAT". He also said, "Don't get me wrong, I want that, but that is not why I am with you." She thought that she was falling in love. *I must get this boy to church,* she thought.

Lizbeth had held something back in that conversation with Jake that day. A big thing. Something Jake might have not understood nor been patient for. She blamed her mother for no "IT", which was partially true, but through youth groups and church she knew God was telling her no to the "IT". God wanted her to wait till she got married. She also was learning God wanted her to be with a guy who was a Christian. Jake was not a Christian. He was a super great guy, but he did not know who God was, had no relationship with God, and didn't go to church. He did not look like the guy in her dream. But now she wanted Jake to be the guy in the dream. PROBLEM....

Looking back, Lizbeth knows she should not have ever dated Jake. Why go through all these feelings of love, only for one or both of you to be heartbroken in the end? But she knew no one would have been able to sell that to her when she was 16 and looking for love. Jake had been the human factor she was longing for. She needed someone to love her, listen to her, care about her, and all those things he did. But Lizbeth knew that Jake was not going to be her husband. She knew this because she kept the promise she made to her father. She never told Jake about the private life of "Lizzie Mitty", and all the things that happen. She knew the man she would marry would get all of her. He would be the person she could share everything with. How would she ever give Jake up? She loved him.

To enhance your experience please pause at this time in reading and feel free to YouTube the following song.

Zach Williams & Dolly Parton, "There Was Jesus"

Every time I tried to make it on my own
Every time I tried to stand and start to fall
And all those lonely roads that I have travelled on
There was Jesus
When the life I built came crashing to the ground
When the friends I had were nowhere to be found

I couldn't see it then but I can see it now
There was Jesus
In the waiting, in the searching
In the healing and the hurting
Like a blessing buried in the broken pieces
Every minute, every moment
Where I've been and where I'm going
Even when I didn't know it or couldn't see it
There was Jesus
For this man who needs amazing kind of grace (Mmm)
For forgiveness at a price I couldn't pay (Mmm)
I'm not perfect so I thank God every day
There was Jesus (There was Jesus)
In the waiting, in the searching
In the healing and the hurting
Like a blessing buried in the broken pieces
Every minute, every moment
Where I've been and where I'm going
Even when I didn't know it or couldn't see it
There was Jesus
On the mountain, in the valleys (There was Jesus)
In the shadows of the alleys (There was Jesus)
In the fire, in the flood (There was Jesus)
Always is and always was
No I never walk alone (Never walk alone)
You are always there
In the waiting, in the searching
In the healing and the hurting
Like a blessing buried in the broken pieces
Every minute (Every minute), every moment (Every moment)
Where I've been and where I'm going
Even when I didn't know it or couldn't see it
There was Jesus
There was Jesus
There was Jesus
There was Jesus

Bye Bye Love

Jake graduated and left for college. As he was only an hour away, he came home every weekend to see Lizbeth. Jake's family adored Lizbeth, they were happy he had reason to come home. Lizbeth allowed herself to get close to his family as well. They knew nothing of her home situation because Lizbeth held her promise to her dad to tell no one. Jake had an inkling that Lizbeth's family was a little off-kilter, but Lizbeth was careful not to tell him the full story. Lizbeth found comfort with Jake's family. His mom looked at Lizzie like she was her daughter. She would share stories with Lizzie and play with Lizzie's long hair. She would braid it and tell Lizzie how beautiful she thought she was, inside and out. His mom would laugh and tell Jake, "You better marry this little gem." Lizzie was sucked right in. This was what a family felt like. She even taught Lizzie how to French braid her hair, sew, and crochet. His sister was amazing, she would sit and laugh with them, give Lizzie advice on boys, and a couple of times they even double-dated with her. Lizzie's time with Jake's family was effortless. She was not on edge and could relax.

Everyone at Lizbeth's school thought they were an adorable couple. Jake would come to school on Fridays because he didn't have classes and walk the halls with Lizbeth. He would hang out with some of his old teachers, while Lizbeth was in class, but be promptly waiting outside the classroom door to walk her to the next class. Lizbeth was a senior now, so she could leave school at 12:00 pm on Fridays. They would hang out until about 5:00 when Lizbeth's mom would pick her up from school. The photography teacher did a photo shoot of them for a photography show she was doing and gave Jake and Lizbeth a copy of one of the more dramatic shots.

It was so cute. Jake and Lizbeth looked like brother and sister. They had the same sun-kissed hair, blue eyes, and bronze color skin. In the photo, Jake was leaning against a tree and Lizbeth stood in front of him while his arms were wrapped around her waist. He was looking down at her and she was looking up at him. In the background, the sun shone through the trees like a star. Lizbeth was in love with the picture and put it on her dresser at home. She could not imagine they would ever break up, even though she knew this was not the person God had set aside for her. She had invited Jake to church many times. He went once, but after that, he said he had to work with his dad on Sundays, so he couldn't go. Lizbeth should have seen the writing on the wall. But Jake was her comfort, she loved hanging out with his family. His older sister was so wonderful to Lizbeth. The sister Lizbeth always wanted. Breaking up with Jake would lose him and his family. A double whammy. NO, she could do it. "Lord, please make Jake a Christian, and let him be the person I marry. Please Lord, I want him. "Only him! I don't want anyone else.", she prayed.

110

Christmas time had arrived. This was never a good time of year for Lizbeth, even with Mom's moods somewhat thwarted, her mom continued with her 20 times-a-year holiday events of episodes. Christmas was always the worse. Lizbeth came home from school; Mom was in the darkened room again. She was crying and was very agitated. Lizbeth went in and made her a cup of tea and brought it into her thinking this might give her some comfort. Nope, tea thrown across the room, a bunch of expletives blurted out. Warning all victims take cover.

Lizbeth learned that something had happened at her mother's work. She had been fired. She apparently lost control with a customer for something, and Mom slapped her real hard and called her a bunch of vulgar names. Mom was back. Dad called it a relapse. She had been in an emotional remission, and now she could not control herself. She even exposed her mood to outsiders, which really showed how bad a state she was in. Now there was going to be a lawsuit. Dad had been called to the police station to come to get her. He got her off with minor charges. Apparently, the officer took pity on him when Dad shared some of the things that happened in Mom's past. He promised he would get her help and medication. So at least the charges were minor, but the woman who was struck was going for blood. She was suing my mother for damages.

Things with Dad and Jake got increasingly distant. Lizzie no longer had time for Dad. No more going to the grocery store. No more watching his favorite tv shows. No more just hanging out to talk. Lizbeth left Dad in the dust, and he was not ok with it. He was pissed. He was a pot of water on the stove that was about to boil over. He was just waiting to have Jake gone. Now, with Mom back to her antics, Dad needed Lizzie and she was nowhere to be found. O wait. She was able to be found, she was with Jake. Jake became the sore that would never heal for Dad.

The week before Christmas and all through the house, not a creature was stirring not even a mouse. With one exception, Lizzie and Jake were in the kitchen, it was late maybe 11:00 and the kissing fest had just commenced. Jake had gotten Lizzie an early Christmas present, a diamond promise ring. He had pledged his intent to marry her someday. Forget what God had said to her, forget he didn't go to church, forget that Dad hated him. Jake wanted to marry her, and she loved him. "God, I want this!, she indignantly prayed, "MAKE IT HAPPEN."

Now, nothing was going to happen more than the kissing fest. Jake was used to going home and taking cold showers, which in a way made Lizzie feel good. She liked how powerful it made her feel. She did not realize how unkind all that was. She just saw it was the way to keep him interested. In fact, it worked, now Jake had given her a promise ring and was talking about getting married in a year. Probably because he wanted to stop taking cold showers. Anyway, Lizbeth was back to doing things her way, not God's way and it was time for not just a smack, but Lizbeth needed to be taken out at the knees. They were at Lizbeth's house remember? Her mother was still making good on the yearly visits, and they were at Lizbeth's house! Dad came around the corner and caught the intensity of their kissing fest, slap, dating restrictions were immediately put into effect. Jake was allowed to see Lizzie, 10 times a year. If he wanted to marry her, seeing if he could stand the heat was Dad's goal. See if he would be true to her then. The reality was Dad just wanted Jake gone, and he used it as an opportunity. The reality was God just wanted Jake gone, and Lizbeth refused to listen. Revelation 3:19 " I rebuke and discipline those whom I love, be zealous therefore repent."

Lizbeth hadn't realized it at the time, but the Lord had been giving her all these little pushes, signs, and prompts to know what His will for her life was, but she was refusing to listen. She knew Jake was not her forever person, but she refused to give him up. She knew there was a huge part of her, her God half, which was growing stronger about now, that he would not understand. How can you give only half of yourself to someone? How can you marry someone if they only could understand half of you? The answer is, You can't. So, when Lizbeth didn't listen to God's plan, He had no choice but to turn up the heat. Lizbeth headed into the boiler room and the explosion was imminent, explode it did, but not before Mom could rub a little salt in the womb.

Jake did try to man up and called Lizbeth's Dad at work. He arranged to meet him, and Dad did show up. But Dad was not looking for Jake to come back. So even though Jake humbled himself and apologized for taking liberties he should not have, Dad's heart was as cold as ice. He apologized for everything he could possibly think of, but Dad was not budging. "Thank you for calling me, I appreciate this was a hard thing for a young man to do. I respect you a lot for that," Dad said. Jake thought he had a chance. He thought he was seconds away from shaking hands and Dad and him having a new understanding of each other. ..... Aaaa nope. Dad continued, "As much as I can see this was a mature thing to do, I do not think you are the right person for Lizbeth, and we will see what a little distance does for both of you."

Drum roll please, Dad had Jake against the wall as the firing squad took their shots. Jake was dead. He lost it. As Jake boiled over, he said unthinkable, and non-reversible things to Lizbeth's dad. He called her dad jealous, and messed up in the head, that he wanted Lizbeth all to himself. Jake ended his diatribe with the final blow, "Lizzie will choose me not you. You will see. I will take her away." So, what started as good intentions, was the nail in the coffin. 10 times a year ended up never again. Duh da da.

Meanwhile, on the home front, Mom was up to her own sick and twisted way of playing with Lizbeth's mind. Lizbeth came home from school; she was anxious because she knew Jake was going to see her dad. She had not heard yet how the talk had gone, so she was on edge waiting for Jake's call, or even better for Jake and Dad to show up and all ok. Yes, that would be it. "Dear Lord. Please let the meeting with Jake and my dad go well. Please intervene for me. Only you can make this right," she prayed.

As Lizbeth arrived at her room, there on the bed was the picture of her and Jake. The picture was ripped in half, her face lay to one side and his lay to the other side, separated by a piece of paper with the writing. "THEY WILL BE NO MORE" written in red pen. All around the crime scene were votive candles burning like a Voodoo curse. Lizbeth flipped. She wanted to hall off and hit her mother, she wanted to tell her exactly what she thought of her. She wanted to tell her, that she never had what she had with Jake. She was going to tell what a terrible wife and mother she was. But then she heard that voice say, "STOP!" She punched her pillow and clenched her fist, inside her head she chanted, *I hate her, I hate her, I hate her.* She fell to her knees and sobbed.

She looked to her dresser, Jake and her picture had replaced the two foldable scripture cards that she had held so dear. They were now tucked away in her drawer. She had done it again. She had not only put God on the shelf. She had tucked him away. Yes, she got it. The hurt still hurt but she had to own her part in all of it. Jake was not for her. She knew it. She fought it. But God had answered her prayer exactly. "Dear Lord, please let the meeting with Jake and my dad go well." It did go well. Someone that was not right for her was taken out of her life. "Please intervene for me." Yep, this was definitely Divine intervention. God did intervene for her. He took Jake out when she did not have the strength to do it. "Only you can make this right". Check box number 3, only God could make it right, because Lizbeth would not have given Jake up on her own.

Her furry subsided and logic set in. She still cried bitter uncontrollable tears, but she knew when Dad got home Jake would be gone. Saying any of those things to her mother, who had returned to beast form, would do her no good. The savior that she thought she had in Jake, to take her away from all this was gone. Jesus was back where he belonged, her Savior, and her looking to Him for help. Her heart was aching like she had never felt before. It felt like someone had ripped her heart right out of her chest. But she knew God had done for her what she could not have done for herself. She wanted her Speed Racer. When would he come? Something told her, Speed Racer would show up when Lizbeth was not desperate for him. When she was ok, that's when God would say she was ready. God was not going to let a guy be her savior. He wanted to know that He was her Savior.

To enhance your experience please pause at this time in reading and feel free to YouTube the following song.

Jordan Feliz "Next To Me"

I've been empty
When I'm low, you fill the cup, yeah
But my ego fights back telling me that
I'm ready to grab the wheel and take control
But I'll crash if I don't let myself let go
You put the "X" on my faded map
Draw me a line back to where you're at
Patient when I try to move too fast
I get this feeling
I get this feeling
I get this feeling in my spirit when I'm low
I hear it calling like a compass to my soul
Saying, child, come on back now
You've been gone too long
Let me lead you back where you belong
Right next to me (me, me-me, me)
Right next to me (me, me-me, me)
I've been captive by the plans I tried to make, yeah
I've been selfish
'Cause callous heart they die hard like habits
That I know I gotta break
Ain't it good to know that help is on the way? (Help is on the way)
You put the "X"on my faded map
Draw me a line back to where you're at
Patient when I try to move too fast
I get this feeling
I get this feeling
I get this feeling in my spirit when I'm low
I hear it calling like a compass to my soul
Saying, child, come on back now
You've been gone too long
Let me lead you back where you belong
Right next to me, oh, oh-oh
You know I tried to do it on my own (on my own)
Oh, oh-oh

You say it's time for me to come back home
Right next to me (me, me-me, me)
I get this feeling in my spirit when I'm low
I hear it calling like a compass to my soul
Saying, child, come on back now
You've been gone too long
Let me lead you back where you belong
I get this feeling in my spirit when I'm low
I hear it calling like a compass to my soul
Saying, child, come on back now
You've been gone too long (back where you belong now)
Let me lead you back where you belong
Right next to me (me, me-me, me)

Freedom, Trapped, Exposed

Lizbeth sat on her bed and read the pages of her High School Yearbook. Page after page students wrote, "You are so nice to everyone." "I wish I could have gotten to know you better." She had secrets, thus she never let anyone get too close. She never wanted to let her guard down, for fear she might let something slip out. She was eighteen now, and off to college. Well, off to commute to college. Her father needed her to help with Mom. So, he forbade her to go away.

Pricilla had been sent away to college in Virginia. Daddy was her purse, and she never came back. This was a good thing, after the firing, and lawsuit, Mom never sought employment again, so things were more peaceful with Pricilla gone. The battle of wills had subsided. Mom did not know enough about Lizbeth to attack her. At this point, Lizbeth played caretaker and no more. She offered no additional affection to her mother. After Jake, she never let her relationship with her dad return to its formal glory. She wanted to find love. She wanted to find her own life and way; she was not going to be his wife forever. She would help him care for Mom for sure, but she never looked at him the same. The jealousy he showed over Jake was sick. She had seen his heart. He wanted her to be there forever. She belonged to him, and he would fight back against anyone who tried to take her from him. So, she decided, I will commute, because you are forcing me to, but I will be on campus as much as possible. And so, she was.

On the first day of freshman orientation, she filled out an application for employment in the registration office and the library. Amazingly she got both jobs. This meant she had to be at school early in the morning before classes to work in the registration office, and late at night to serve in the library. Dad did not buy her a car, although he did get one for Pricilla. She was reduced to him driving her and picking her up. Lizbeth thought this is going to be short-lived; she would buy her own car. Dad knowing her need to have freedom and separate from him, put limitations on this milestone. The car had to be brand new, for "Safety" reasons. He did not want her to break down. Her determination to obtain a car, her FREEDOM, was so strong in addition to taking 18 credits she worked 40 hours a week between the two jobs.

By the end of her freshman year, she had saved enough money to buy a brand-new car. She found the perfect gem; an Isuzu I Mark. She saw it at a mall show and loved it, so she approached her dad declaring she was ready to buy a car. Dad reluctantly took her to the car dealership but hoped that Lizzie would be left wanting. He knew her finances to afford this car were riding the line, and to his pleasure she was two hundred dollars short from closing the deal. Dad was thrilled; he had bought some time. He had another month with her under his thumb. Dad had no idea how much

Lizbeth wanted her FREEDOM, as he was packing up and ready to head out the door, Lizzie turned to the salesman and said, "Is there another vehicle within her price range?" The salesman said he had the same car, but it did not have air conditioning. He assumed no one would want a car that did not have air conditioning. Lizbeth made the deal and bought the car of her dreams without air. She was used to being in the fire. A little heat for a few months in the summer was definitely better than being chained to her home.

Lizbeth loved her job in the library. At night she killed 3 birds with one stone, socialized, got her work done, and was paid for doing it. She worked at the main desk and checked out books. Not too many books were getting checked out, and most students came to study, or socialize. At the registrar's office, she gave tours in between classes, sent out invitations to prospective students, and called those students to remind them a representative from the college was coming to visit their high school. It was great. Touring made Lizbeth high profile without her realizing it. As she paraded around campus, in a skirt and high heels, boys noticed, girls also noticed, ones in the sororities. The sorority girls were surveying the campus for new recruits. Unbeknownst to Lizbeth, it would be on a tour, her "Speed Racer" would notice her, and vow that she would be his. This would not be until her senior year; Lizbeth still had some hurdles to jump over.

By the end of freshman year, she had saved enough money to buy, yes, a brand-new car, be on the watched list for 2 sororities, and catch the eye of her next boyfriend. That was the upside. She also endured heartache of course. What is life without a healthy dose of heartache? Heartache is God's Avenue of grabbing our attention. Every time she forgot herself, and thought, I got this, God was able to step in and move her out of the way of herself. She felt tired most of the time, school, work, and home she had nothing left to give. *Mathew 11:28-30 "Come to me, all you are weary and burdened, and I will give you rest."*

The home front barely affected her now. She got home late, still being picked up by her dad at this point, she would come home to clean up her mother's feces, yes feces off the floor, make dinner for dad, then he would allow her to take the car and go back to school for her job at the library. To get attention, these days mom resorted to urinating on the floor or going #2. Lizbeth saw her mother was sick, like who does that? Yep, a kook, crazy person, Lulu, nut job, these were some of the adjectives Lizbeth thought of when it came to her mom. Other than that Lizbeth was not home much, by her design. Dad was lonely and she could tell, but she could not think about that right now. She had given enough of herself over the years, and now she needed to make sure she made a life for herself, or she would not have a life. She knew for sure she was not meant to be Dad's companion forever. Dad's repugnant feelings toward Jake revealed to Lizbeth that her dad had no intention of ever sharing her.

In addition to all her activities, Lizbeth joined the FCA (Fellowship of Christian Athletes). They met on Saturday nights and their studies into God's words were exciting. Quiet Lizbeth was now the one who had something insightful to share with the group. She met some nice girls and all of them were more than generous to share their dorm room with Lizbeth. One even gave her a drawer where Lizbeth could keep toiletries, change of clothes, and other items so she did not have to cart them around in her backpack. No one knew her troubled past, nor all the responsibilities that awaited her when she was home. All they saw, was an impeccably dressed (due to her tour job), smiling, friendly girl who was perky and exhumed the appearance that she had everything. Lizbeth learned to make friends without letting them get too close to the inner her. All her friends would have said they were her best friend, but Lizbeth did not know how to let anyone in, in order for them to be best friends. She knew how to fake it. Lizbeth's final height was 5'1 with an all-time high weight of 93 pounds. She was a little squirt and on the surface was easily looked at as a pushover.

This persona is what led her to the first debacle. Her math teacher, an older man in his late fifties, bucked-toothed, with thick glasses, pot belly, and receding hair that stood up like Einstein, was notorious for trapping his freshman students into nefarious activities to earn them higher grades came on the scene. He was often seen in the early morning hours just as the sun was peaking over the horizon sashaying out of the girl's dorm. YUCK. *Who would do that kind of thing?* Lizbeth thought when the rumors crossed her ears during lunch with the girls. He was repulsive looking. "Who would do him?" Lizbeth blurted at the table. All the girls laughed. *People think I am funny* she thought. Well, kind of? It was just so unexpected that something like this would come out of Lizbeth, so for that reason yes, she was funny. Coming from a world of high school, where she was quiet and flew under the radar, Lizbeth was experimenting with her wit. She did not want to be that girl that people said, "You are so nice to everyone, wish I could have known you better." So, in an attempt to leave that girl behind she tried to be bolder, witty, and noticeable.

Noticeable, if she knew how she was going to be noticed, she would have struck that from her list of things she wanted to be. Lizbeth saw herself as innocuous. She was certainly no Marilyn Monroe. She was Skipper, Barbie's little sister. She had an innocence about her that was apparently intriguing to a dirty old man. Yes, the one and the same "math teacher". The first week of classes he took a shinning to Lizbeth. Even though he had a reputation, Lizbeth thought she was immune to his advances. She looked like a child. Well, dirty old men apparently like children. Gross. So, one day when she was struggling with several new concepts in math, with the test around the corner, she decided to go for math tutoring to none other than, "The Molester", the teacher who was seen coming in and out of the girl's dorm early mornings.

She went to the professor's office during office hours to see when he was available. He was already assisting another student with the door closed. That was the first warning that she missed. Teachers do not have office hours with girls with the door shut. DUH. On the door was a sign-up sheet and she saw he was available in an hour. She scribbled her name and needing a pick-me-up, decided to go grab a cup of coffee to hold her over. When she returned, the door was open, and he was sitting at his desk. In she went like the lamb to be slaughtered.

He motioned for her to have a seat, he promptly got up and closed the door of his office. Mayday, Mayday, Houston we have a problem! Lizbeth? Nothing on her radar, dumb little shit. If you were watching a horror movie you would have been screaming for her to look up and get out. But no, Lizbeth was too busy rummaging through her notes to see the cat that was preparing to eat the canary. Fortunately, Lizbeth's life to this point, had made her "Tweety Bird." Tweety Bird always got away from the cat and so did she. As he corned her in his office and ran his hand down her leg, nervousness set in. Lizbeth knew…. *Crap… think fast… don't show fear… be faster….be smarter…outwit the fox.* Lizbeth dropped her folder on the floor so he would have to remove his hand. Then she got up with one twirling motion and reached the door. He was up and ready to pounce. He pinned Lizbeth against the door and moved in for the kill. Quickly, she reached her hand behind for the knob, "Please Lord, let the door be unlocked. Help me get out!" she prayed. The door was unlocked, but he had her pinned hard against the door, his weight was too much for her. "LORD HELP ME!"

Knock... knock... knock.... Someone was at the door. Yes, it was enough of a surprise that he was thrown off guard and Lizbeth yanked the door open and out she sprinted. The gazelle had escaped the lion's jaws. She never looked back. She never told on him either. She did not want to be known as the girl who was attacked by "that" teacher. That was not what she wanted to be known for. She promptly dropped the class and resigned that she would take it another semester with a different teacher. She did tell a couple of her friends, wanting the rumors of him to flourish so other young unsuspecting girls would not be taken off guard. And that was that. Lizbeth brushed off the dust and moved on with life like nothing ever happened.

It was clear, God, showed up, Again. He had a way of clearing the path, just when she needed it cleared. She went to FCA that night and her accolades for her Saviour were even more exuberant. She never shared all the logistics of what led to her acclamations that night, but the others saw her joy and shared in her acknowledgment that He shows up when you need it most. Mathew 6:8 "Your Father knows what you need before you asked him."

To enhance your experience please pause at this time in reading and feel free to YouTube the following song.

Kings Porch, "I Speak Jesus"

I just want to speak the name of Jesus
Over every heart and every mind
I know there is peace within your presence
I speak Jesus
I just want to speak the name of Jesus
Till every dark addiction starts to break
Declaring there is hope and there is freedom
I speak Jesus
Your name is power
Your name is healing
Your name is life
Break every stronghold
Shine through the shadows
Burn like a fire
I just want to speak the name of Jesus
Over fear and all anxiety
To every soul held captive by depression
I speak Jesus
Your name is power
Your name is healing
Your name is life
Break every stronghold
Shine through the shadows
Burn like a fire
Shout Jesus from the mountains
Jesus in the streets

Jesus in the darkness over every enemy
Jesus for my family
I speak the holy name, Jesus
Shout Jesus from the mountains
Jesus in the streets
Jesus in the darkness over every enemy
Jesus for my family
I speak the holy name, Jesus
Shout Jesus from the mountains
And Jesus in the streets
Jesus in the darkness over every enemy
Jesus for my family
I speak the holy name, Jesus
Your name is power
Your name is healing
Your name is life
Break every stronghold
Shine through the shadows
Burn like a fire
Your name is power
Your name is healing
Your name is life
Break every stronghold
Shine through the shadows
Burn like a fire
I just want to speak the name of Jesus
Over every heart and every mind
I know there is

Lizbeth had a way of just letting things go. Perhaps the development of that skill helped her survive her mother's antics. Consequently, the next day it was like nothing ever happened. However, after the teacher nightmare, Lizbeth was looking for a little fun. Life could not just be all work and aggravation. So, when her friend begged her to go to watch the men's basketball game, she thought it would be a nice relaxing time and she could catch up with her friend Janet.

Janet was in love with this one basketball player, Steve. He was Janet's Greg. Lizbeth knew this feeling well, but she also knew the reality of the situation. Janet noticed everything about Steve, but Steve did not even know Janet existed. As she talked and talked about Steve this and Steve that, Lizbeth felt bad for her. Janet read something romantic into everything Steve did. If Janet passed Steve on campus, she would say, "He changed his route to classes to see her." If she made sure she was behind him in the dining hall and their hands brush against each other she would say, "He was trying to touch her hand." On and on she would go. In Janet's mind, Steve and she were minutes away from dating. Even at the game when Steve looked their way, Janet implicated it as an attempt for him to gaze at her. Janet enjoyed the sympathetic ear of Lizbeth, so the routine began, Janet pulled Lizbeth to every basketball, for moral support.

Now Lizbeth who arrived on campus early every day often saw Steve leaving the girl's dormitory in the mornings. She often saw him with multiple girls, and when he was with his guy friends, well, he was an ass. She did not know how to break the news to her friend that the man of Janet's dreams was not worth a "cat nap." Lizbeth started to point to other guys to refocus Janet's attention saying, "He is cute." Nope, Janet would go right back to thoughts of Steve.

The night of the basketball tournament arrived; Lizbeth could not make it to this game. Janet went with another friend. This friend not knowing the facts, encouraged Janet to make Steve a special candy bag and to wish him luck at the game. She pushed Janet to go up and give it to him. Janet was nervous she could not speak. When Steve said, "Oh Wow, what's this for?" Janet said. "Oh, my friend told me to give it to you." Steve smiled and said, "Hey thanks, I'll catch you after the game, I want to ask you something." THAT WAS IT! Janet could barely contain herself. It was finally happening; STEVE was going to ask her out, she thought to herself, he said, "I want to ask you something." She could not hold in her happiness. She cheered louder than ever. She screamed Steve's name to cheer him on, after all, she was going to be his girl.

The game ended and Janet sat on the bleachers waiting for Steve to come over and ask her out. She was beside herself. Steve did eventually come up to her, sat down, and said, "Hey tell your friend thanks for whole candy thing." Janet was not thinking clearly and thought he was trying to say, tell your friend thanks for pushing you to do the candy thing. Of course, she thought, it was the whole candy thing that led them talking. Janet giggled and flirted just waiting for him to say more. AND HE DID! "So, your friend is that cute little blonde that comes to the game, right?" he said. WAIT? There was a shift for Janet. Something was wrong here, what is he saying? She thought she must be hearing wrong. NOPE! Steve continued, "Do you think you could set us up?" OMG, on no he didn't. He what? He is asking her!. Her Janet.... To fix him up with Lizbeth? How could this be? Couldn't he tell she liked him? Hmmmmmm Janet's humiliation and anger now turned to Lizbeth. WHAT did she do? She must have flirted with him. She did something. What a little bitch. All this time she comes to the game for me....... Ha, it was for her, Lizbeth wanted to snake her Steve. How could she do this to me? Janet snapped her attention back to Steve when he said, "Well? Will ya?" "Oh sure, I will talk to her, and see?" Janet recovered in front of Steve he suspected nothing. "I will definitely talk to Lizbeth," Janet said. That was exactly what Janet planned to do, she was going to give Lizbeth a piece of her mind. As soon as she saw her for breakfast tomorrow, she would rip Lizbeth apart.

Lizbeth had had a rough night; she was not able to make it to the game because her mom was at an all-time low. Dad was working late so Lizbeth had to stay with her mom for suicide watch. Her mother often from time to time would threaten to kill herself. When these episodes happened Dad always called Lizzie to be home, so Mom was not alone. Neither Dad nor Lizzie ever thought Mom would actually do anything to herself, but you never know.

The suicide watch turned to violence when Mom got something in her head that Dad was late from work because he was having an affair. By the time Dad came home, Mom was fit to be tied. She lunged at him punching him in the head and chest and arms. Dad never hit her back but did defend himself by grabbing her wrists. She spat in his face, calling him really horrible adjectives. This was nothing new for Dad and Lizzie, it had all happened multiple times, but Lizzie was tired, and her spirit was not as perky as normal. She really needed a break from life, to be honest. No, Lizbeth never considered suicide since she was 13 and God showed up, but she was tired of living.

Life was just so hard all the time. Long story short, the punching continued, mom got hold of a knife, tried to stab her dad, Lizzie got in the middle. She and Dad were able to get the knife out of her hand, now Mom lay panting on the floor. Mom was foaming at the mouth, and she was speaking in a horribly demonic tone. Lizzie suggested to her dad that they pray over her mom; so, they did. Mom screamed in pain, "You're burning me", and continued to blurt out curse words, which even turned into words of blaspheming the name of Jesus.

This was a lot. Lizzie thought she was in the middle of a horror movie. She wondered if Mom was demon-possessed. As Lizbeth continued to pray, Mom took the heel of her hand and hit Lizzie in the jaw. Ouch. Then Mom struck her in the ear with the other hand. She grabbed the front of her shirt and ripped it. Then mom started the sick laugh, Lizzie knew too well. Lizzie continued to pray, and Dad did too. Mom settled down; Lizzie and Dad were spent. Mom then curled into a little ball and started to talk in a little girl's voice. This was a new side of her mother. Lizzie had always seen the mean one that cursed, she saw the happy fun mom all giddy, and now she was a little girl talking in a little baby voice. Lizzie turned to her dad and said, "We can't do this anymore Dad, you have to get her help! Mom has at least 3 multiple personalities. We cannot handle this on our own." At this point her dad had assumed his normal position of sitting with his face in his hands, this time he was shaking his head back and forth. As bad as Mom had been over the years, and as violent as things would get, this whole personality thing was over the top. Dad and Lizbeth got Mom up to bed and Lizzie covered her with a blanket. Mom would sleep for days now after this ...... Lizzie kissed her dad on the forehead and said, "I love ya Dad, I'm sorry!" she walked away holding back tears, she truly felt sorry for him, but she resolved that this was not going to be her future. She knew somehow, someway, she would have to leave Dad behind. She felt guilty for being so selfish, but at the same time justified that this was not the life God intended for her.

The next morning Lizbeth assessed the damage to her face from the blows it took the night before. There was a slight bruise on her chin started, and her ear had a gash in it, where Mom's nails must have ripped into it. She could cover her ear with her hair, and her chin she would have to come up with an excuse. OK, she tripped walking up the steps and banged her chin. That works she thought. She readied herself and left to meet her friends for breakfast before she had to go to work. Lizbeth liked going to the dining hall. She never ate much, but social time with friends was like an escape for a while. She could feel like a normal girl when she was at school. She could pretend that she had a normal life and a normal existence.

But Lizbeth knew she did not have a normal life or existence, not because of the dysfunctional home she resided in, but because of the way the Lord reached out to her. Why? She often asked. Why Lord did He give me such a showing of Himself? When she was younger, she used to think maybe she was His favorite. After all, she wanted to be like David, A girl after God's own heart. As she grew spiritually the answer came loud and clear. The Lord showed up, the lord revealed his spirit to her only and only because she asked. She called on HIM. She asked for HIM. She wanted HIM. God wanted a display of our love for Him. Something her Sunday school teacher had told her, God wanted all of us. He wanted us to have a relationship with Him. He wanted us to talk to Him about everything and anything. He wanted the good, bad and the ugly in us, and in return He would transform us into the good, the redeemed, the washed clean. Only God could do this.

To enhance your experience please pause at this time in reading and feel free to YouTube the following song.

Zach Williams, "Stand My Ground"

Oh, oh oh oh oh oh, oh oh oh oh
Oh, oh oh oh oh oh, oh oh oh oh
I'm done, I'm done
Done with who he said I was
I'm free, I'm free
For he don't have a hold on me
No, I'm not gonna cower
I'm not gonna flinch
I'm not gonna run from this
I will stand my ground
Ain't no way I'm backing down
When that devil comes around
I'm gonna stand my ground
Fight, I'll fight
And even if it takes all night
I'm stone, stone cold
And nothing gonna shake these bones
I will stand my ground
Ain't no way I'm backing down
When that devil comes around
I'm gonna stand my ground
And I will stand my ground
And ain't no white flag waving now
And when that devil comes to town
I'm gonna stand my ground
No, I'm not gonna cower
I'm not gonna flinch
I'm not gonna run from this
No, I'm not gonna cower

I'm not gonna flinch
I'm not gonna run from this
I will stand my ground
Ain't no way I'm backing down
When that devil comes around
I'm gonna stand my ground
And I will stand my ground
Ain't no way I'm backing down
And when that devil comes around
I'm gonna stand my ground
And I will stand my ground
Ain't no white flag waving now
When that devil comes to town
I'm gonna stand my ground

Lizbeth arrived at breakfast; she was her perky self even though she was walking a tightrope. She was on the edge, between the pressure of school, work, friends, and MOM, she had hit her limit. Lizbeth was not prepared for what happened next, and neither was Janet for that matter. Janet had gotten to breakfast early; her plan was to confront her backstabbing friend as soon as she arrived and before the other girls got there as well. So, when Lizbeth sat down, Janet struck hard and fast. She relayed the night's events with venom and sneered at Lizbeth with snake-like eyes. There! Janet was content, Lizbeth had remained silent, while Janet's entire diatribe against her friend spewed out. Her parting words to Lizbeth cut to the core, "You just think you are so special. You have everything! Everything just happens for you! You have the best life, and you prance around so happy all the time, it's because everything goes your way! What would you do if you had a bad day, you would probably be destroyed. Well, some of us don't feel pretty. I hate how you just have the best life." Lizbeth just starred at her like a deer in headlights. Tears welled in Lizbeth's eyes; Janet felt she had accomplished the belittling of her "ex-friend". Janet was the victor and Lizbeth was left speechless, or so Janet thought.

And just like that, Lizbeth struck back. She did not yell; she did not become angry. She looked at Janet with a look of sadness and said, "You think I have a perfect life? Do you think everything goes my way? Let me tell you............" Lizbeth did it, Janet's venomous attack was the straw on the camel's back. Lizbeth emptied herself in giving Janet a full picture of her night last night, the professor, her mom's episodes, and why she commuted to college the whole nine yards. Yes, Lizbeth finally burst and told all. Janet's face looked like she had been slapped. It was slapped, slapped with the truth. Janet did not know what to say. She knew it all had to be true because no one could make up that shit. Lizbeth ended her emotional release by saying she had no interest in Steve, she would have never even considered him, one because he was an ass, and second because of how her friends felt about him. Lizbeth got up and left the table, hurt by her friend, guilty she broke her promise, and FREEEEEEEE. Lizbeth finally told someone her version of hell. It felt good. She had never told anyone and now the floodgates had been opened. How does she close them now when she knew how good it felt to open the gates?

It was Sorority pledging time, and sororities were sending their invitations to those girls they thought best fit the persona of their sorority. Lizbeth received two bids to pledge. One from Tau Sig, which was known for athletic girls, and one from Phi Psi which was known for the preppy girls. All of Lizbeth's friends got bids for Phi Psi as well, and that was the sorority Lizbeth wanted to pledge. At this venture in her life, she did not want to be an outsider looking in, but she knew it was impossible. Her dad was still picking her up from school at 5:00, she was going home, doing her home thing, and then driving back to college to work in the library. She had no time to be a pledge, and she did not drink. Her FCA friends were all against fraternities/sororities and questioned her desire to associate with such groups. All Lizbeth knew was that she did not see it that way. She wanted to be a good witness to others, she didn't see how you could be a good witness if you were hidden away and never interacted. You had to be in the trenches.

PHI PSI was the group she wanted to be part of, so she decided she had to be honest with her feelings. She scheduled to meet the President of the sorority and told her that she loved the girls in the sorority and that all her friends were going to say yes to their bid, but sadly she had to decline. There was Oh No, why? Lizbeth opened her heart and advised how she had two jobs on campus, and in between that, she went home to care for her sick mother. That's all she shared; no promise broken! She added, "I don't drink, it would be unfair to the others". Lizbeth had heard that during "Hell" if there was a pledge that did not drink the others had to make up double for that pledge. The leader looked at her bewildered, no one ever just told the truth, not like that. She had never experienced someone pose a scenario that looked out for others' feelings. She hugged Lizbeth, and that was that. NO sorority for Lizbeth, or so she thought.

Lizbeth made up little treats for the pledges to help them get through hell week. When they stood on the wall and had to do embarrassing things for onlookers to see, she was there to cheer them on. The evenings she was on campus, she was there to clean up their throw-up when they drank too much, get them coffee, or put them to bed. She was their little Mother Theresa. The pledge mistresses at first sneered at her for helping the pledges, it was the pledge mistresses' job to make their lives living hell. But this irritation for Lizbeth's support quickly turned to admiration. Here was a girl who was going to get nothing from her efforts. She was not going to be a member of their sorority, not going to be part of their sisterhood. Why would she do all this? This gained Lizbeth great respect, and her loyalty was seen as sisterhood material.

The secret ceremony of induction was at hand. All her friends were getting ready and so excited. Lizbeth did feel a little left out, but she acted happy for her friends. At 4:30 before Lizbeth left campus an invitation was left at the library for her. It was inviting her to see the induction ceremony.....great.... Lizzie gets to see her friends have everything she wanted. It was bittersweet though, no outsiders were ever included, Lizbeth would watch her friends rally to be in a sisterhood all while she watched, but it was still an honor. She really wanted to say she couldn't make it, but she knew that was jealousy speaking. She had to be there. Although it was tough to juggle getting back to campus when her dad knew she wasn't working, Lizbeth lied and said she had a project at school and a friend was going to let her sleep in her room. Her dad said yes, he did not let her take the car, but he drove her back to campus. Lizbeth felt a little guilty for lying but justified that it was not a lie, she did have a project she had to be at. Proverbs 6:16 "The Lord hates sin regardless of how people try to represent their wrongdoing."

The induction ceremony began, happy for her friends, and sad for herself, was the order of the day. After all the girls got up and received the secret handshake, their ceremonial embrace, and their insignia ring, there was a pause. The leader got up, "We have one more sister to include", she announced. All the girls smiled and turned to look at Lizbeth. They were giving her an honorary membership, for her loyalty, honesty, and integrity. Honesty? Integrity? ... ouch that hurt. Lizbeth remembered the lie she told her father in order to be there. Lizbeth smiled, she was shocked, honored, and remorseful for the lie. How quickly the lie came too. It was easy. There would be more lies in the future as Lizbeth fought to have her own life and escape the entrapment of her parent's dysfunctional arena. She learned, falsely, that the only way she could escape was to lie. And so, she did.

There is a price to pay for sin. There is always an unseen consequence. We won't reap the consequences immediately, but when they mount up, it is a bitter pill to swallow. It would be years before Lizbeth would swallow that pill, but when she did, she had to nail it to the cross. Lies beget lies. Satan's tactics to bring us down are never covered in muck. His schemes look good, make sense, and seem justified until we are insnared. Satan cultivated Lizbeth to become a very skilled liar. Proverbs 12:22 "The Lord detest lying lips, but he delights in people who are trustworthy." In the end, when Lizbeth finally saw how the lies had separated her from God, how the lies changed who she was on the inside, she knew it was only God who could break them. Years later she would pray, "Lord cause me to be a horrible liar, juggle my tongue to prevent me from being skilled to execute them, take from my mind the craft to concoct them." And so, He did. John 14:13 "And whatever you ask in My name, so that the Father may be glorified in the Son."

Now having read Lizbeth's story to this point, some of you might feel Lizbeth was justified to lie her way out of her family's abusive life. You might even cheer for her. Lizbeth believed the same. Every time she lied to her dad to rid herself of their chains, she felt justified. She became cold to her parent's debilitating life. What she didn't see was that every time she had compassion for them, served them, even though they did not deserve it, and forgave them for their offenses, the Lord was teaching her to be more like Him. Taking those elements out of life, stopped the learning. Lizbeth stopped growing in her relationship with Him during this time. So, when the warning came, that this new guy in her life was not for her, He was not her "Speed Racer", she ignored it.

Dylan was a man. He was a junior, and Lizbeth was still a freshman. He had a manly face and a cunning foxy smile. In fact, when Lizbeth first saw him, her first thoughts were, *Oh he is a player. Stay away from him. He is up to no good.* Her second thought was, *he will be my end.* Because of the lies she was telling her dad; she did not see that the original thoughts of Dylan were from God. Her warning! which she gave no heed to, were true. Satan was God's most beautiful angel, sin is attractive, not scary. Dylan was just like that, enticing. Lizbeth was drawn to him like flies are drawn to poop. When he looked at her, it was like he was looking right through her. He was smooth, he presented himself as a Christian, but read no bible, attended no church, and showed no fruit of salvation. Lizbeth was a sitting duck, without Christ having her back, she was taking a swan dive into an empty pool.

It was springtime, all the dogs were on the prowl. Dylan asked Lizbeth to go to his fraternity dinner with him. At first, Lizbeth was going to say no, but one of her friends, Sue, was going and begged her to go. Reluctantly, she agreed. She was nervous. He was much older, and very experienced in the girl scene. He was living the college life and enjoying all its fruits. Lizbeth was a conquest. Who could bed the nun? was the actual bet. There were warnings; Lizbeth chose to ignore them.

The night came, and Lizbeth had a blast, they danced and talked, he was a perfect gentleman. When it came to good night, he hugged her, and that was it. She would have thought him disinterested, but as he left, he asked if they could see each other again. All the warnings subsided, and she was excited. Maybe he liked her? Dylan asked her to meet him the next morning for breakfast. *So nice*, thought Lizbeth, maybe the rumors are wrong. He was a perfect gentleman, and he didn't even try to kiss her, much less anything else.

The next morning, she met him for breakfast. He was wearing a mint green golf shirt that matched the color of his eyes. He was handsome, she thought, more manly than she had liked in the past, but he was also sweet. His voice was smooth and calm, and he carried himself like an athlete. He was ... sexy. He moved like a jungle cat. What was she thinking he was a jungle cat. He was playing the game of cat and mouse, guess who was the mouse? The charmer was after his prey.

After breakfast, they walked around campus together. He gently leaned over and whispered in her ear. "I would like to hold your hand, my lady, if that is ok with you?" My lady? Is he a prince? Swooned Lizbeth allowed his hand to slip into hers. His hand was soft. Her dad would have said, he doesn't work. As they walked along campus, Dylan brought her hand to his lips and kissed the top. Wow, smooth, she didn't realize that he was parading his prize for all to see. He had met her for breakfast, to give an intimation that they had spent the night together. He was making sure the campus was witness to their outing, hand holding, and the suave kiss on the hand was for show. Dylan was setting the stage that he had "Bagged the Nun."

Oblivious to it all, Lizbeth leaned into his shoulder and hugged his arm. The fraternity brothers in on the bet were sold, Dylan had given them enough proof that he had done the nasty with the Nun. She had been deflowered, and he got a notch on his bedpost and a bountiful booty of $200.00. Lizbeth got nothing, but a smeared reputation and a lesson well learned. Or so you might think? To seal the deal, as they ended the walk about campus, Dylan cupped Lizbeth's face in his hands and leaned down for a kiss. Wow, what a kiss. Lizbeth was dizzy. Her first kiss with Jake was not like that. Dylan's lips melted into hers, it was like their lips were made to kiss each other. It was passionate, yet respectful, just long enough to not offend her. Her legs felt like they were about to buckle. He was indeed a skilled kisser. As she pulled away to end the kiss, he was still holding her face and their eyes locked. He looked bewildered and confused. He shook his head, and with a smile said. "Did the earth move?" Lizbeth laughed, rolled her eyes, and said, "I bet you say that to all the girls." With that she turned to walk away, she looked back to see if he was still standing there, he was. His eyes were glued to her, she flipped her hair, gave him a cute smile, and continued walking.

Wow! "Oh, what a night, late December back in 63. What a very special time for me. What a "man" What a night." That's the song lyric that came to mind as she went into the dorm room to visit her friend. It was then Lizbeth's bubble of delusion burst. Her friend had learned about the bet. Lizbeth was furious. It was all an act. He wanted it to look like they had spent the night together, and his on-lookers were paying up. Lizbeth was pissed beyond pissed. "What are you going to do" her friend questioned. Lizbeth responded, "Just watch and see!"

It was now dinner time, most of the campus would be at dinner. At least most of the fraternity brothers would be anyway. Lizbeth was beyond nervous, she was mad. She had been injured, but more importantly, her reputation had been compromised. Submissive Lizbeth, willing to lie down and take it was gone. She was going to stand up for herself. Think, Lizbeth, think, she thought. Don't be rash. You will look like a woman on the warpath. A woman scorned. You will be a laughingstock. Calm down, take a deep breath, you want him to look like the fool, not you. She centered herself, she had played this act many times, pretending to be ok when all she wanted to do was die.

She entered the dining hall, and all eyes were on her, or so she thought. She slowly walked to the table where Dylan dined. He turned and saw her, with a smile on his face, he grabbed her hand and kissed it. She did not pull it away. He was still playing his little act! Why? She had heard that he already got paid. There was an empty seat next to him and she took it. This had to be executed perfectly. She had to play him in front of everyone. She was surprised he could not see the contempt in her eyes as she looked at him. No, he was in full fledge acting mode. He was attentive and sweet, acting like he was love-struck. *What an ass*, she thought. She leaned into him to whisper in his ear, and the whole table around them whispered and awed. "Awwwww Dylan", they chanted. He was beaming ear to ear; Lizbeth had helped him with his rouse. He leaned closer to try to hear what Lizbeth had to say. She said, "So I hear there was a little bet?" Dylan's face turned white, and the smile turned serious, he looked her in the eyes and was speechless.

Lizbeth stood up. She smiled at all the guys at the table. They were mesmerized. She had command of the room. "So,

146

gentleman, I hear that you all have been cheated?" They were listening. She smiled at each one as she made eye contact, a flirty smile, to suck them all in. "It is sad when someone cheats a stranger, but much worse when someone cheats their brothers, don't you think?" Dylan was out of his seat now. He put his hand up for Lizbeth to stop, she was not going to stop, but she yielded for a moment. Dylan looked at his fraternity brothers and said it. "Most of you know that there was a bet." He looked down at Lizbeth to indicate that he was sorry. She was in no mood for a cowardly sorry. "I did not win the bet", he continued. "Oh, come on", someone yelled, "We saw you love birds around campus, we saw you at breakfast this morning", they cooed. Dylan put his hand up to say stop again. He said, "Yes, I did that on purpose so you would all believe that I had won the bet." "But I didn't take the money. I told them, I didn't win the bet."

What! Lizbeth was shocked. Wait! he could have collected the money and didn't? No, Lizbeth don't get sucked in, she said to herself. What kind of a guy would make a bet like that in the first place, she thought. He is not for you! Jeff turned right then and there to her and said, "Lizbeth, I am sorry, you are the classiest girl I have ever met." He turned to the whole dining hall, and yelled, "I didn't win the bet. I am the biggest Jerk!" He looked over at Lizbeth with his mint green eyes looking like a pitiful puppy and whispered, "Lizbeth, I truly am sorry." Well, that was it. It was all a farce, but at least her reputation was salvaged. Lizbeth shook her head, indicating ok, turned and left the dining hall, while her sorority sisters cheered and whistled at her victory. Lizbeth had done what no other girl had done. She had confronted her assailant, and he caved.

Days went by with no sightings of Dylan. *Good,* she thought, but that is not really how she felt. She avoided her normal routes around campus so as to not run into him. Sure, he had confessed, but he still did it. And what about the damage? She was hurt, she had been played. She thought he really liked her. It hurt. At least, she was not dealing with sneers and whispers about her. In fact, people she didn't even know were slapping her hand, as a show of support. Then she thought about Dylan. If she was getting a show of support, he was probably getting trashed. Good, serves him right and any other guy who has done that. The thing was, she wondered if he was ok. She liked him and knew she shouldn't. Thoughts kept creeping into her head like, he was a big person to admit it. He never did take the money. He didn't have to make an announcement to the whole dining hall. Satan was enticing her to think of Dylan fondly, getting her sucked into excusing him, missing him, wanting him.

The next day Dylan's friend was waiting outside one of her classes. He was waiting for her. He approached her carefully; He knew she was a force to be reckoned with. He said, "Can we talk?" "Sure, she said, "but here, in the open." She did not want to get caught up in another scandal. He continued, "You know Dylan is really sorry about what happened." "Well, he should be, you all should be. I am sure I am not the first girl you guys did that to," she stood her ground. He hung his head and didn't answer. That was the answer enough. Yes, they had done that before. This was just the first time a girl didn't just lie down and take it. Who would have thought that the girl who took so much abuse growing up, had changed so much? Where did all this resolve come from? Lizbeth had no idea, but she liked this new Lizbeth. She was not a victim anymore. She was her own defender. She was her own protector. She was her own way-maker. She didn't realize it, but Lizbeth had put God on the shelf again. SHE, SHE, SHE.... not HE, HE, HE. Lizbeth had lost her way again, and Satan was on the prowl. Lizbeth was traveling on dangerous ground, and she had taken her greatest protector and put him out of commission.

Dylan's friend continued. "See the thing is, He told me that morning, he was canceling the bet. He didn't take the money. He planned on paying his end of the bet that day before you even came up to him." Wait? What? His end of the bet. Lizbeth stopped in her tracks, she turned to Dylan's friend and asked, "What was his end of the bet?" she asked. "If Dylan lost and didn't .... Well, you know.... He had to announce to the whole dining hall that he lost. Which of course he ended up doing", his friend pointed out. "Ok, so, he lost the bet, and he did what he was supposed to do. Whatever! it is over now." Lizbeth said. "No, you don't get it, Dylan didn't know that you were going to oust him, he was planning on doing it himself", his friend pushed as if there was more to the story. "OK...AND?" Lizbeth said. "Don't you get it? His friend countered. "He called it off, cause you mean something to him. He hasn't felt like this toward a girl since his ex from high school dumped him. Lizbeth, He really likes you. He didn't want your reputation damaged. He cared," his friend charged.

"OK, so what, Dylan finally likes a girl? I am supposed to be all giddy about that?" Lizbeth barked. "Whatever! said his friend. "I just thought that you should know. I thought maybe you should give him a chance.", his friend walked away leaving Lizbeth standing there with her mouth hanging open in shock.

"What should I do?" Lizbeth asked Sue, her best girlfriend at the time. "WOW, if I had a guy that cared that much, I would snatch him up. I think you are stupid if you don't forgive him. I would totally go for it." Lizbeth would learn that Sue was no friend. In fact, Lizbeth would discover that Sue knew about the bet before she talked Lizbeth into going to the dinner with Dylan. She not only knew about the bet, but she bet against Lizbeth. She bet Dylan would win.

Softened by her friend's urgings, Lizbeth was primed by the time Dylan showed up at the library one night while she was working. All anger and hostilities had been averted. She wanted to see Dylan; she had wanted to run into him. In fact, the thoughts of him invaded her mind every second. Interestingly, Lizbeth never asked God what to do. She never revisited the thought of her dream of Speed Racer. If she had she would have concluded that Dylan did not fit the bill. Just like Jake was not her Speed; Dylan was not her Speed either. But she didn't pray, she listened to the rantings of her unsaved friend. She did not run the whole scenario through a God check. She was trusting herself, and her own thoughts and feelings. This served as a dangerous cocktail.

That night in the library, Dylan said all the right things. First a million I'm sorry's, followed by, he once was in love, and a girl crushed him. La Di Dah. He never allowed himself to really have feelings for someone after that... La De Dah... But, he had so much fun with her. When they slow danced that night, he got goosebumps and didn't want the night to end. He didn't kiss her good night cause of the bet. He didn't want their kiss to be wrapped in the bet. He called the bet off that morning before breakfast... La De Dah. So, when they did kiss it was real. When he asked her if the Earth moved, it wasn't a line. When his lips touched hers, it was like their lips were made to kiss each other. She was made for him. Hook, Line, and Sinker... Lizbeth was sold. She took the bait, Satan had her on the hook. He had reiterated the exact emotions she had felt. Dylan was her person!

Dylan and Lizbeth were official. They were a couple and went everywhere together, seen on campus walking hand in hand. The skeptics eventually became fans. Those who thought Dylan was a jerk, eventually thought they made a cute couple, and had a really cute story. Lizbeth was in love again. But he was not her Speed Racer, which she had never considered. She put the Speed Racer story out of her mind and cast it off as just a dream and not a promise of her future.

One year later, Dylan ended up cheating on Lizbeth with none other than Sue, her best friend. Dylan confessed to his mistake and Lizbeth forgave him. As for Sue, Lizbeth and she were no longer friends. When Lizbeth tried to talk to Sue, Sue cut her to the core. Sue challenged Lizbeth and told her. If she was not going to put out and satisfy her man, another girl would. See Sue had always liked Dylan, but he was never interested in her. She encouraged Lizbeth to be with him, so Sue would have access to him as well. Once Dylan relaxed around Sue, she took advantage of a night he had too much to drink, and Lizbeth was nowhere around. She knew Lizbeth was struggling with being physical with him, so she jumped at the chance to seize the moment. Scorned, by Dylan, who called out Lizbeth's name, Sue was out for vengeance. If she had any say, and she did, Dylan would not end up with Lizbeth.

Lizbeth was a mess. Again, she did not think of God. She had drifted so far off kilter. Lizbeth had hoped Dylan was going to be her savior and take her away from her home situation. He would marry her. She had to forgive him. She had invested so much time and energy. Plus, she was in love with him. Although Lizbeth forgave Dylan, it didn't mean she condoned the offense. Truth be told the trust she had in him was gone. She would never trust him again.

Distrust and growing arguments with Dylan over Lizbeth's family put the nail in the coffin. Dylan and Lizbeth ended long before they ended. Lizbeth's heart started to harden when Dylan, knowing only small details of her mother's illness, pushed her to give up her family. Yada, Yada, Yada, he cheated again with someone else and was such a coward he broke up with Lizbeth over the phone. Lizbeth was devastated. She had forgiven him before, how could he? But she knew God was yanking her back to Him. She had lost her way again.

In these moments of despair, she basked in God. He gave her strength. He gave her peace. Why did she always let her relationship with Him slide? It was a slippery slope, when things were bad, she clung to Him, and then as soon as she got the desire of her heart, on the shelf He would go. Ouch, how she must make Him feel in those moments. She would have definitely given up a relationship like that. What did God get out of it? She would close her eyes and imagine Him crying every time she discarded him like an old rag. She didn't feel that way about him, but the cycle was the same.

Again, she asked her Why? She knew how great the feeling was when she was so deeply connected to Him, why would she give it up? "Picture Him crying", she said to herself. When she started to drift, she pictured Him crying.

The problem was the drift was not conscious, it was subtle, it happened slowly; she'd miss a day and then another day talking to Him. It always ended the same, she would get herself into another debacle and He would come to the rescue. How exhausting for Him. *He must roll his eyes at her she thought.* UGH, she didn't want God rolling His eyes at her. She wanted to be David. She wanted to be known as the girl after God's Heart. "Lord, I want you to look at me and see I am after your heart. Close all doors that take me from you. Take Satan out so he can not distract me and rob me of all the time I could be seeing you in my life. Open my eyes every day to see your hand in my life." And so He did.

To enhance your experience please pause at this time in reading and feel free to YouTube the following song.

Unspoken, "Mistakes"

I make 'em, I try to hide 'em
Sometimes it feels like I'm defined by them
All of the evidence stacked against me
All of the fingers that are pointed at me
I can't deny it
All of my mistakes

Woven through my story
All the mess I make
God, use it for Your glory
Every wrong turn, it's true
Led me right here to You
I may lose my way, nothing's greater than Your grace
Not even my mistake
Not even my mistakes
I hunger to be holy
But I still wrestle with the old me
You know who I am, who I'm becoming
Through all the dirt and the stains, you love me
I can't deny it
All of my mistakes
Woven through my story
All the mess I make
God, use it for Your glory
Every wrong turn, it's true
Led me right here to You
I may lose my way, nothing's greater than Your grace
Not even my mistakes
Not even my mistakes
Every hard fall, back in yesterday
Every stumble that I've yet to make
The cross redeems, and washes them away
And washes them away, oh
All of my mistakes
Woven through my story
(My story, oh)
All the mess I make
God, use it for Your glory
(All for You, Lord)
Every wrong turn, it's true
Led me right here to You
I may lose my way, nothing's greater than Your grace
All of my mistakes

(My mistakes)
Woven through my story
(My story, Lord)
All the mess I make
God, use it for Your glory
(Oh God, use it, Lord)
Every wrong turn, it's true
Led me right here to You
(You)
I may lose my way, nothing's greater than Your grace
Not even my mistakes

Life without Dylan was unbearable. Or was it? Was it Dylan she missed or was it the fact that she was alone? In desperation, she broke down, "Lord why did you take Dylan from me? Please give him back. I will do anything if you give him back?" The answer was, "He was never to be yours in the first place." Wow, that hit her hard. She knew it was true. She remembered how they began. She remembered her first thoughts of him, O*h he is a player. Stay away from him. He is up to no good. He will be my end.* She remembered her dream; Dylan was not her Speed. Literally, he was not her speed. This was her fault. She did it to herself. She opened her world and her heart to someone she knew, in the beginning, was not for her. She did not heed the warnings. God let her go. He let her do things her way. He knew how it would end. He knew she would be broken. He knew He would meet her there. So, He rescued her again. She prayed, "Lord, I'm sorry. I am a mess without you. I mess everything up. I need you. Forgive me. I want what you want for my life. I want to do it your way. I surrender. I don't want to date again until I meet my Speed."

Lizzie's Speed

Time passed and Lizbeth was going to be a senior in college. It was August. In the Summers she worked full-time for the registrar's office. Graduation was on the horizon and life choices had to be made. Lizbeth's journey with God was back on track. She had remained single. She wasn't looking for someone to save her. She had her Lord to do that. She was trusting Him with her future. She was giving a tour of the campus and never even noticed, John. He was unloading his car and moving into his dorm house, as she passed by him, the wind caught her hair, he heard her voice and her laughter as she directed the prospective student around the campus. "WOW", John said to his father, "I wonder if all the girls look like that. I am going to be dating that girl." Lizbeth walked by and didn't notice John.

Over the past three years, Lizbeth had made a guy friend named Bob. He was great. They talked all the time. He would take her out here and there, he was always dating a bunch of girls. He was quite the gigolo. Lizbeth considered liking him, he had confessed over and over that she was the girl he was going to marry. He wanted to have his fun now, but when it came down to marriage, he wanted a girl like Lizbeth. It was always said as a joke, but the truth was Lizbeth knew too much about Bob to ever consider him.

To her he would always be her friend, and anything other than that, well, YUCK!

By senior year, Bob and Lizbeth got closer and hung out all the time. John was a freshman and lived in the same dorm as Bob, he had become Bob's sidekick, and where Bob was so was John. Lizbeth did not give it a thought, but John was positioning himself to be with Lizbeth. He wasn't Bob's side kick he wanted to be Lizbeth's sidekick. John was not her type at all. He had black hair, light eyes, slender build, he drove a Camaro (big turn-off for Lizbeth, flashy cars were not for her), and hehe, he wore driving gloves. *Who wears driving gloves?* Lizbeth thought. John was also a freshman and Lizbeth was a senior. She would never consider having a relationship with someone three years younger than herself.

The day came when Bob told Lizbeth that John wanted to ask her to a fraternity dance, Lizbeth laughed; Bob and she made a joke about it and that was that. John never asked her to go but continued as Bob's sidekick. Lizbeth was unaware, but Bob knew John's intentions, and although he never thought John would have a shot with Lizbeth, Bob was not taking any chances. Bob told John that Lizbeth laughed at the thought of it. Embarrassed, John never asked her to the dance, nor did he go. *Potential threat averted* Bob thought. Bob was ready and was aligning himself to be with Lizbeth. He had had his fun and now he was a senior, he would not let Lizbeth slip through his fingers, especially not to a freshman.

Lizbeth got used to John's presence. She never considered him as dating material, but she did notice that he was very mature for his age. He had a heart that was ripe for God. He was curious and when things came up in conversation and Lizbeth would share something about God, John was listening. Bob was rolling his eyes. Bob knew that Lizbeth was a bit of a "God Freak", he was raised catholic, but never understood the relationship factor required with God, so in his mind although sometimes annoying, the "God quality" would make Lizbeth good wife material. Lizbeth kept taking notice of John's character. He was different. He was a smart aleck, but kind and very gentlemanly. He dressed terribly, like the Italian Stallion with a gold chain around his neck, a ring on his finger, and silk shirts. OMG, he looked like John Travolta in *Saturday Night Fever*. Nope, definitely not Lizbeth's type, but a super nice guy.

One weekend, Bob had gone away, and Lizbeth found herself hanging out with John. They talked and swapped stories. Lizbeth was able to see beyond the exterior of him. She saw his heart. He asked if he could go to church with her. And so, he did. In the next two weeks, John became Lizbeth's sidekick. She liked him, but she was struggling with his age. She could get past the driving gloves and the way he dressed, but he was a baby. She was a senior, plus she vowed that she was not going to date until it was real. John confessed that she was the first girl he had seen on campus way back in August and that he didn't really like Bob, but he knew he could see her if he hung out with Bob. They talked about God and Lizbeth shared how special God was to her, and John was all in. He said he was always looking for something more, just never found it. John became saved and John and Lizbeth started dating.

Lizbeth's girlfriend, was tired of hearing John this and John that and she finally said to Lizbeth one day, "Well when am I going to meet him?" Lizbeth arranged for John and her girlfriend Amy to meet the next morning at breakfast. That morning John and Amy met. Lizbeth was anxious to have her friend's opinion of John. She was still apprehensive about dating him because he was 3 years younger than her and where could it go? So, when John went up to get some more food, Lizbeth seized the moment and drilled Amy for her thoughts and opinion of John. "What do you think?", Lizbeth prodded Amy. Amy looked at Lizbeth, made a face, and said, "He looks like Speed Racer. Amy saw Lizbeth's far-off look and said, "Do you remember that cartoon?" Amy laughed. Yes, Lizbeth knew the cartoon well. "What did you say?" Lizbeth gasped. She needed to hear it from her friend's lips again. "He looks like Speed Racer, don't you think?" followed by laughter from her friend.

Lizbeth felt like she was in a time warp. She never saw it, this whole time, she never made the connection, the driving gloves, the black hair, light eyes, slender build, the Camaro. Why had she been so blind? John fit the bill. Yes, John did look like Speed Racer. More importantly, Lizbeth had never told Amy about the "Speed Racer" dream. This was a God thing. God was showing up again. He was sending her a message, John was it. Lizbeth then told her friend the whole story. Her friend looked at her and ghast. "Wow, that's scary! You think God talks to us like that?" Amy asked. "Yes, I do." Lizbeth said and gave Amy the salvation story. That afternoon Amy became saved, and John became Lizbeth's speed. Her Speed Racer. Lizbeth kept the whole "Speed Racer story" to herself and never told John until the day he asked her to marry him and she said, "Yes." Lizzie and John were official. As they strolled along campus, John wrapped his arm around Lizzie's waste turned, and gave her a kiss, Lizzie's foot instinctively popped up behind her and Lizzie felt safe. She said, "Thank you God for bringing me my Speed." As she opened her eyes she saw them, no it couldn't be, she squinted her eye to focus better. There in the parking lot, parked under a tree were "The Eyes."

"But the Lord stood by me and strengthened me, so that through me the message might be fully proclaimed, and all the Gentiles might hear it. So, I was rescued from the lion's mouth." 2 Timothy 4:17

Epilogue

Lizbeth found her Speed Racer, but the Lord was not done with her. She was to endure more emotional steppingstones in her journey. As her walk approached the horizon of a life free from the emotional abuse of her dysfunctional family, her family fought back with a furry. Lizbeth would not be robbed of the life God wanted her to have, but she had to fight for it. She also longed for a mom figure in her life. She had been deprived of having a mom, tasted it briefly with Jake's mom, and craved for more. God would show Himself again and again in her future. See how her life unfolds with Speed, as well as how God turns tragedy into her calling to adopt a child and save them from a life of abuse.

Christ sees us not full of impurity, but full of potential. He in the refining imagery, is the refiner and we are the lump of unrefined gold, full of impurity and full of potential beauty. Sometimes we expect God simply to zap the junk out of our lives when we enter into a relationship with him, but it is more of pressing. He squeezes it out, and in the pressing, there is often pain. The result is the formation of that precious metal which had to go through the furnace in order to be formed.

To enhance your experience please take the time to YouTube these final songs.

Bethel Music & Kristene Dimarco, "It is Well"

Grander earth has quaked before
Moved by the sound of His voice
And seas that are shaken and stirred
Can be calmed and broken for my regard
And through it all, through it all
My eyes are on You
And through it all, through it all
It is well
And through it all, through it all
My eyes are on You
And it is well, with me
Far be it from me to not believe
Even when my eyes can't see
And this mountain that's in front of me
Will be thrown into the midst of the sea
And through it all, through it all
My eyes are on You
And through it all, through it all
It is well
And through it all, through it all
My eyes are on You
And it is well, it is well
So let go my soul and trust in Him
The waves and wind still know His name
So let go my soul and trust in Him
The waves and wind still know His name
So let go my soul and trust in Him
The waves and wind still know His name
The waves and wind still know His name

And it is well
With my soul (sing it out)
It is well
With my soul
It is well
With my soul
It is well, it is well with my soul (sing it out, it is well)
Oh, it is well (it is well)
With my soul (because of who You are Lord)
Oh, it is well
With my soul
It is well (oh)
With my soul
It is well, it is well with my soul (sing it out, it is well)
It is well, it is well with my soul (it is well, it is well)
It is well, it is well with my soul
And through it all, through it all
My eyes are on You
And through it all, through it all
It is well, Lord
And through it all, through it all
My eyes are on You
And it is well with me

Carrollton, "Made for This"

I take a breath, I'm not gonna lose
This is what I came here to do
I walk that wire and I take that step
Won't look down, got no regrets
Won't look down, got no regrets
I was made for this
I was made for this
Born in the wild
Formed in the fire
Built for the battle, oh

I was made for this
I was made for this
Mind over matter
Silence the doubters
I have the power, oh
I was made for this
I don't give up, I won't back down
Goodbye worries, no time to doubt
I feel the power, I won't be afraid
Fear won't stop me, I don't break
I was made for this
I was made for this
Born in the wild
Formed in the fire
Built for the battle, oh
I was made for this
I was made for this
Mind over matter
Silence the doubters
I have the power, oh
I was made for this
I'm a soul on a wire
That's where I feel alive
Open up the skies
I'm a soul on a wire
That's where I feel alive
Open up the skies
I am free to fly
I was made for this
I was made for this
Born in the wild
Formed in the fire
Built for the battle, oh
I was made for this
I was made for this
Mind over matter

Silence the doubters
I have the power, oh
I was made for this
I was made for this